Mapping
Responsibility

Mapping Responsibility

Explorations in Mind, Law, Myth, and Culture

HERBERT FINGARETTE

With a Foreword by Robert C. Solomon

OPEN COURT
Chicago and La Salle, Illinois

To order books from Open Court, call 1-800-815-2280 or visit
www.opencourtbooks.com.

Cover image © 2004 by Andrew A. Hasse. Reproduced with permission.

Open Court Publishing Company is a division of Carus Publishing Company.

Printed and bound in the United States of America.

Library of Congress Cataloging-in-Publication Data

Fingarette, Herbert.
   Mapping responsibility : explorations in mind, law, myth, and culture /
Herbert Fingarette.
     p. cm.
   Includes bibliographical references and index.
   ISBN 0-8126-9564-X (trade pbk. : alk. paper)
   1. Responsibility. I. Title.
   BJ1451.F48 2004
   170—dc22
                                                              2004007150

*To my wife, Leslie, whose long labors
deciphering my versions and many revisions,
whose keen and rigorous editing of every line,
and whose loving support amid the many
ups and downs, made this a precious
sharing of our life together.*

Contents

Foreword

Herbert Fingarette has long been one of the most original and provocative philosophers in America. His explorations into the questions of self and responsibility go back to his classic book *Self-Deception*, which already prefigured his emphasis on taking (and not taking) responsibility. His book about Confucius, *The Secular As Sacred*, dared go where few Sinologists had gone, to explore Confucius as an actual philosopher. He took on the refusal to accept responsibility by way of victim mentality in his heretical book *Heavy Drinking*. In this volume, he revisits these steps of his career in some delightfully succinct and up-to-date essays. Self-deception, Confucius, and alcoholism share the table of contents with Fingarette's usual sensitivity to Freud and psychoanalysis, the notion of "nonaction" in the Bhagavad Gita, the question of punishment as retribution, the definition of mental illness, a meditation on suffering, and another on the book of Job. But throughout, the focus remains on taking responsibility. He does not allow himself to get tangled (except for one chapter) in the free will versus determinism problem. And he begins the book not with a paradigm case of responsibility but with the disturbing case in which someone lacks any sense of responsibility at all. Fingarette then asks, how do we develop such a sense? This is a wonderful book, bringing together some of the best thoughts of a bold and distinguished thinker.

—ROBERT C. SOLOMON

Preface

This book represents some fifty years of exploration of the theme of responsibility. I have done this from a variety of standpoints. Each chapter offers soundings in depth, not an abstract general theory.

When I speak of responsibility here, I do not mean causal responsibility, when "Who is responsible for that?" simply means, "Who caused it?" The latter question is a purely factual one, not a philosophical one.

The philosophical question is the one that poses problems. How can we explain moral responsibility? What is necessary to be a responsible person, that is, one who is justly held accountable, blameable, perhaps punishable? Is this a question peculiar to our modern Western culture, or does it make sense in every culture? Why is it that some who are causally responsible for what happens nevertheless not be held morally or legally responsible, not held accountable or blameable? Whence comes the authority that ultimately justifies and even demands holding people to be responsible agents? The questions are many, and the answers often elusive.

Not surprisingly, then, some of these chapters view responsibility from the standpoint of moral psychology, psychoanalytic psychology, and psychology generally. However, others develop topics in criminal law in connection with criminal responsibility, retributive punishment, and coercion. In addition, several chapters take up the themes of the great Aeschylean tragedies of ancient Greece, the teachings of Confucius, and the teachings of the Hindu Bhagavad Gita, which provide still other, radically different points of view on personal responsibility.

Responsibility is commonly said to depend upon having a free will. Consistently with current theory in physics, however, I have argued that we can be responsible even when what we will is a matter of chance.

The chapter on suffering provides a very personal view of the paradox of activity and passivity that pervades preceding chapters. It also offers entry to the final chapter, which deals with the ordeal of Job and his epiphany through suffering.

In each particular field I chose issues that intuitively seemed to bear on the topic. But the challenge in each inquiry was to think in ways distinctive of that field. A number of the chapters were originally published in the relevant specialist literature (as indicated in footnotes in the relevant chapters). In this work, however, the general reader constitutes the audience. Therefore, these previously published chapters have been substantially revised. My object has been to spare the general reader text, notes, and jargon that were desirable for the technical statement but unnecessary and burdensome for the serious nonspecialist.

Some of the chapters appear here for the first time, and they have been written at the outset with the general audience in mind, though they are based on rigorous background research.

For me this has been (and remains) a fascinating journey. In offering these essays, I do so with the belief that the general reader will find this a journey into regions that offer fresh and original insights.

Accepting Responsibility

Becoming Responsible

A four-year-old boy finds a box of matches. He enjoys playing with them. He sets fire to a neighbor's wooden building. He does this not out of spite or dislike of the neighbor, but for the pleasure of it. He knows it is considered to be wrong, "naughty," forbidden. The adult who left the matches lying around might be held morally or even legally responsible for the damage. But the child, though he may be punished, is not a morally responsible person.

Well, then, when will the child become, morally speaking, a man? What age is that? It is surely less than the legally responsible age. A seventeen-year-old would be morally responsible for the same act, yet he would not normally be responsible before the law.

In general, when and how does a person become morally responsible? Philosophical answers to this question have commonly focused attention upon the circumstances of the action in question. "Did he do it?" "Is all behavior 'determined'?" "Was he free?" "Did he know what he was doing?" "Did he intend to do that?" "Could he have helped doing it?" "Are there any excusing or mitigating circumstances?"

Other answers have hinged on the question of whether the person ought to be blamed, punished, or in some way held accountable for the action. "Does he deserve punishment?" "Will blaming him alter

This is a revised version of an essay that originally appeared in *Mind*, n.s., 75, no. 297 (1966): 58–74, with the title "Responsibility."

his character or conduct?" "May he be called upon to answer for what happens?" Still others have supposed that moral responsibility turns in some way on some combination of the preceding issues.

I shall devote myself here, however, to showing how a fuller understanding of moral responsibility takes one much closer to what Kant called "the extreme limit of moral inquiry," the question why men should will the moral law.[1]

The gist of the answer is that acquiring moral responsibility does not just happen. Responsibility must be accepted. As a practical matter, by a certain age the individual is normally expected to accept responsibility. This acceptance is evident if there is genuine care or concern of the kind which is peculiar to moral responsibility. There are many marks of such concern beyond the obvious—caring behavior. There may be inner moral conflict, self-restraint, remorse, guilt, or other such manifestations.

Now what if this acceptance of responsibility and responsible care do not appear in an adult? What if we found some villain who was rational, but who had no inner response to the moral qualities of human beings? In other words, suppose he were morally blind. He might be very knowledgeable about moral issues in the way that a blind person could be knowledgeable about what is going on in the art world, but not having the capacity to respond to the artistic values of the art work.

It might seem that unless our villain has one or another of the acceptable sorts of excuses, he is responsible for what he does. This, I think, is error. Were we to be convinced that our villain really had not accepted moral responsibility, that he really did not care in the appropriate way, we would neither in justice nor in fact hold him morally responsible. And I shall begin the systematic argument for this thesis by presenting some extreme and clear-cut illustrative material from the practical world.

Irresponsibility and Psychopathology

The current edition of the American Psychiatric Association's Diagnostic and Statistical Manual (DSM-IV) estimates that overall an average of 3% of males are diagnosable as having an Antisocial Personality Disorder.[2] This diagnosis roughly corresponds to what was once called psychopathic or sociopathic personality. The most distinctive of the relevant traits is a casual disregard for and violation of the rights of others. Consistent irresponsibility is a key attribute.

Let us put aside what might be the cause of such a person's troubles, and let us look instead at what he is and does. Here are some principal characteristics drawn directly from the DSM-IV: Those with antisocial personality may express themselves with a glib charm, verbal fluency, and superficially impressive technical knowledge. They may be self-assured, even cocky, and may thrive in polemical or legal dispute. They tend to be consistently irresponsible. They are exploitative and promiscuous in sexual relationships. They are readily deceitful and manipulative in quest of profit or pleasure.[3]

What can one do with such a person? Well, what do people do? After all, the psychopath is not a rarity. This is particularly true among the prison population and among others who are repeated offenders against the law.

The usual first response is what we might expect: those around them try to hold them responsible. Their glibness and apparent sincerity, their social skill and their ability to get friends and parents to make restitution for them often lead to light punishment or to forgiveness for their misdemeanors. Eventually, those who have followed their careers—parents, friends, police—come to appreciate that they are incorrigible. Their life of irresponsibility is not one of defiance of moral values. It is a life that is chaotic from any moral standpoint, an incoherent life in the quest of momentary gratification.

The cumulative effect of their antisocial acts, or perhaps some more flagrant criminal venture, leads to their indictment on a serious charge. If the opportunity for probation or dismissal by a skillful show of contrition will no longer do, their defense may take a radical turn. The defense attorney may bring up the long, sorry record and use it as a basis for a plea of "insanity." Legal confusion in this area has been endemic.[4]

Regardless of the special concerns and tactics of the law, it is evident that almost as a matter of definition anyone who conducts himself this way is not morally responsible. It is pointless to consider him or treat such a person as genuinely morally responsible.

Confusion arises in the courts because of failure to recognize that the acceptance of responsibility is an independent moral development. It is mistakenly assumed that rationality is the sufficient condition for responsibility. This has led to the persistent debate in legal circles over the critical problem of classification and treatment of the psychopath.

I would now like to examine separately, and in greater detail, the notions of "accepting" and "caring" as used in the present context. Then I shall turn again to "moral responsibility," and consider various distinguishable ways in which we use that phrase and its close variants.

Accepting

Certainly, explicit statement of acceptance is not necessary. "Martha, will you marry me?" And Martha blushes, sighs, throws herself wordlessly into your arms, and embraces you rapturously. It will be a specious defense later if she argues, "But I never said 'yes.'" Acceptance usually needs no special words—only an intelligible history of act and circumstance.

There are times when one does accept responsibility by uttering some characteristic "performatory" utterance of the sort, "I accept responsibility for. . . ." But these are occasional and special forms of acceptance, and they get their force in special contexts. I have said that acceptance of responsibility may be and usually is tacit, but we should not confuse tacit acceptance with merely advancing in age. This common error results in part from the fact that usually acceptance of responsibility is inextricably embedded in a long history of complex patterns of conduct. Yet in our self-consciously philosophizing moments, we easily tend to overlook the acceptance as such because it is not localizable in some single act or well-defined course of conduct.

For example, I am morally culpable if, not having given my wife forewarning, I do not show up for dinner, remain away from home until late, and cause her grief and anxiety. I am responsible for being home reasonably promptly. Yet I never explicitly announced I would be home for dinner on this night, nor did I ever make some explicit but general commitment to the effect that I would always be home for dinner. I just do come home every night for dinner. Though this, considered in isolation, establishes no responsibility, when taken in connection with other features of my home life, it all adds up to the fact that I have accepted this responsibility.

Why should I speak of acceptance here? Should I not rather say I just become responsible? To see why it is appropriately called acceptance, one must consider the following. At any point in my domestic career I could have acted otherwise than I did, often without betraying any of my responsibilities at the time. Had I acted differently, my responsibilities would often have had a different form. I could have arranged that if I were not home by an hour before dinner, I would not be expected. Or I could have simply established a pattern of intermittently coming home late for dinner. This behavior alone would tacitly indicate that I do not accept responsibility for arriving promptly.

Of course, tacit acceptance—and, for that matter, explicit acceptance—requires a certain mastery of our social practices. I must know what I am doing, though I do not have to think of it consciously or be perfectly clear about it. How much one must know is a question to which we will return later.

A certain resistance to the idea that acceptance is necessary to responsibility has its roots in child-rearing practices. With children, our interest is to make them aware of the nature of the responsibility they must accept if they are to become full members of the community. It is with this attitude that we would scold and punish the little boy who set the fire. It is a characteristic technique of education for moral responsibility that when the individual is judged mature enough to accept a certain degree or kind of responsibility, we treat him much as if he had already done so. We praise, censure, appeal, obligate—in short, we hold the youth responsible. It is in the nature of the human being that, if we have chosen our moment well, the response to this treatment is actual acceptance of responsibility. In this pedagogical context, it makes sense to speak of holding someone responsible even though this precedes the individual's actual acceptance of the responsibility. Yet even in this context we do withhold our judgment that the child is genuinely morally responsible until we see the signs of genuine acceptance of responsibility.

Caring

Care and concern are inextricably connected with having accepted responsibility. We recognize acceptance of responsibility only if we see its expression in responsible care. So, too, we understand responsible care not as moved merely by whim, or taste, or liking, or affection, but as an aspect of the acceptance of responsibility.

Acceptance, care, and responsibility are part of a family of terms that form a quasi-autonomous idiom within a language. It is in the context of this language and its use that the concepts take on their distinctive significance.

Should not those who are otherwise rational and healthy persons be held responsible, whether they care or not, for doing physical or mental injury to a person out of mere whim? One wants to say: morality is not a game! One has a right to pull out of a game at will. But certainly this can't be true of the moral life!

Pronouncements such as these come readily to mind, deeply tinged with feeling. Our moral earnestness is evident. But what we have in mind is not evident. Are we now contemplating an actual situation of the relevant kind? Is what we have in mind the situation where a responsible person acts irresponsibly? Of course it is true that a person who has accepted responsibility is blameable for irresponsible conduct. What is in question here, however, is the person who has in fact never accepted responsibility—the child, the psychopath, and perhaps the psychopathic dictator who orders killings and torture with no acceptance of moral responsibility and hence no sense of guilt.

There are, after all, real-life nonresponsibles, either the full-blown psychopath or those with psychopathic (irresponsible) tendencies. These individuals do often evoke outbursts of righteous intolerance. But, alas, those who must deal with such individuals must eventually face the reality. The surrender of our moral expectations of such individuals is not a surrender of our moral concern. The case is akin to our having moral concern for the child even though we do not expect the child to have the capacity for responsibility. It is like expecting the blind person to appreciate the work of art by direct observation.

Moral Responsibility

We are now in a position to see how an individual may be held responsible in some particular matter although even tacit responsibility for it had not been accepted.

The man who walks by his neighbor's empty house and sees the driving rain pouring through a door blown open, who neither shuts the door himself nor bothers to mention it to the neighbor when he meets him in town—such a man is not legally responsible for the damage, but surely he had a moral responsibility in which he was remiss. If he claims, upon being censured, that he has never explicitly or even tacitly accepted responsibility for concern for his neighbor's house, we discount this. We do not reject his plea because acceptance of responsibility is unnecessary. We think he really did, somehow, tacitly accept that specific responsibility. We take this stand because he is a responsible person.

In becoming a responsible person, we tacitly engage ourselves to take responsibility in a vast range of situations, many of which cannot be predicted beforehand. The responsible person is one who has learned to identify a reasonable variety of these situations even though they may not have been previously imagined. He knows the ropes, though there is no rule book.

"He knows the ropes." Or does he? Not always, not infallibly. He may cry, "I never took responsibility for my neighbor's house!"—and then we must call him to his responsibilities. "You should have!" we reply. In so saying, we may be simply bringing the obvious to his attention. In other, less obvious cases, we may in effect be arguing for what we judge to be a reasonable extension of personal responsibility.

A significant part of life as a responsible person consists in coming to learn the scope of one's responsibility. We accept more than we at first realize. There is nothing self-evidently wrong about the notion of learning what is entailed by what we had previously accepted. Parallels are plentiful. We learn from logical operations the unsuspected implications of our axioms. We learn from experience that the unexpected is to be expected. We learn from legal analysis that the contract we signed makes us responsible in unsuspected ways. In short, there is no clear line between not realizing what one has genuinely contracted to do, and not being under contract at all.

In the end, it is our own gesture that decides. But we must take responsibility for the consequences.

Guilt and Responsibility

Freud said,

> Obviously one must hold oneself responsible for the evil impulses of one's dreams. What else is one to do with them? . . . if, in defence, I say that what is unknown, unconscious and repressed in me is not my "ego," then . . . I shall perhaps learn that what I am disavowing not only "is" in me but sometimes "acts" from out of me as well.[1]

Freud was talking here of the adult dream. What he says about the dream he also says in more general terms about our mental life as soon as the superego is established. There ceases to be "once and for all any difference between doing evil and wishing to do it."[2] It should be remembered that Jesus also said: "Whosoever looketh on a woman to lust after her hath committed adultery with her already in his heart" (Matthew 5:28).

Freud's comments must be understood in the context of individual moral development. He holds that the move from the morality of the child to that of the mature adult comes when one faces one's own guilt and accepts responsibility. There has been chronic misinterpretation of Freud on these issues. On the one hand, psychoanalysis has been conceived as antipathetic to religious morality. It has been presumed that the psychoanalytic war cry is "Down with the repressive,

---

This is a revised version of chapter 4 in H. Fingarette, *The Self in Transformation* (New York: Basic Books, 1963).

burdensome conscience!" The corollary of this attitude is a supposed hedonistic bias in Freud.

A specific aim of this chapter will be to show that (1) there is a moral outlook with respect to guilt and responsibility that is compatible with the data and theories of psychoanalysis but that (2) this moral outlook is not a hedonistic one. For example, G. A. Paul, in discussing the moral significance of psychoanalytic therapy, states that the analyst helps the neurotic "[see that he] has not done what troubles him and could hardly have avoided the wish to do it, and that therefore he has no ground for his feeling of desolation and so in part to escape it."[3] Paul's statement implies that the feeling of guilt (feeling of desolation) is reduced by showing the patient, among other things, that he has done no wrong act but simply has wished to do one, and could not help having the wish. It also raises three interconnected questions: (1) Do wishes merit less guilt than acts, all other things being equal? (2) Is the guilt in such cases as Paul indicates therefore unwarranted or disproportionate? (3) Is the primary object of such therapy to reduce or eliminate guilt?

Let us consider the first question. Does an evil wish merit less guilt than the same wish put into action, all other things being equal? My answer is no; wishes count as acts so far as guilt is concerned. Putting the wish into action has consequences that may in their own right be morally bad. The wish to kill, for example, merits a certain guilt. It is the character of the wish and the degree of its acceptance that are relevant to the person's guilt.[4] Executing that wish, though it adds no guilt, is a rough practical indication of the degree of the person's acceptance of the wish. In addition, the deed ordinarily adds to the guilt a series of bad consequences, such as pain and mental suffering. Finally, the deed also acts as a symbol. It is an inescapable reminder of the guilty wish. It presents dramatically and enduringly the fact that the guilty wish is a deep-rooted part of the self. The act may also produce legal guilt and social sanctions. It thus prolongs and makes more permanent the conscious guilt. But the spiritual guilt is in fact no greater.

Let us leave, for the moment, this dogmatic statement of my thesis and proceed to a consideration of question (3). Is the aim of therapy to remove guilt or at least to alleviate it? It is often supposed that this is so, but the point needs careful examination.

From the psychological standpoint, said Freud, "we have from the very beginning attributed the function of instigating repression to the moral and esthetic trends in the ego. . . ."[5] From this it follows that to reduce the sense of guilt would be to weaken the repressive (i.e., moral) forces. But to do this alone would make it more probable than before that the evil wish would in fact be expressed in a deed. This is therapeutically and morally bad.

True, repression is often an irrational means of suppressing evil impulses. As a consequence, the aim of analysis is to remove (some) repressions. This, however, does not imply the removal of guilt. For if irrational repression is given up, but the wish remains, the result of successful therapy will be rational and conscious guilt that curbs the wish. Freud said: "Analysis replaces the process of repression, which is an automatic and excessive one, by a temperate and purposeful control on the part of the highest mental agencies of the mind. In a word, *analysis replaces repression by condemnation.*"[6]

In the previous quotation, "excessive" refers not to the degree of guilt but to the scope and rigidity of the repressive process.

From the preceding, it is apparent that it could not be the objective of therapy simply to remove the sense of guilt for evil wishes. From a therapeutic standpoint and from a moral standpoint, such a result could be disastrous. The guilt associated with an evil wish is an important element tending to prevent the realization of that wish. Thus guilt plays its constructive role in relation to wishes and prior to acts.

This thesis is congruent, as we have seen, with the (Christian) moral view that "whosoever looketh on a woman to lust after her hath committed adultery with her already in his heart."[7] A similar emphasis on the wish rather than the deed lies at the heart of the Hindu and Buddhist outlooks. Thus, the thesis I am now arguing may strike the reader as harsh or unreasonable, but it cannot be fairly charged that it is eccentric.

The ultimate objective of psychoanalytic therapy, and of morality, is to remove both the wish and its attendant guilt. This is accomplished in the final analysis by removing or transforming the wish. This in turn eliminates the guilt. It is not a case of eliminating feelings of guilt, where justified, but of removing the reason for guilt.

We must now consider whether the position expounded by Paul can be supported by holding that the guilt is disproportionate to the circumstances. There is a sense in which neurotic guilt-feelings are indeed disproportionate. As Paul suggests, the therapist does point out a mistake on the part of the neurotic. Yet here we must ask, a mistake in what way? Surely, for example, the wish to destroy someone who is near and dear to one is evil in high degree. Yet this wish is typical of unconscious wishes which trouble many a neurotic person.

The "disproportion" here is not in the guilt for such a wish, but in the wish itself. It is the wish which is childish, irrational, unwarranted: in a word, disproportionate. What is characteristic of the neurotic is his reaction to some situations with just such childishly intense and wild feelings or impulses. These would result in patterns of behavior that are too gross, extreme, or misdirected to achieve any rational objective. That is why the wishes are repressed. What is necessary—from either a moral or a psychoanalytic standpoint—is to modify or to eliminate the wish.

Superficial consideration might suggest that a neurotic person will sometimes feel tremendous guilt, apparently for some ordinary and respectable wish—for example, the wish to disagree with a parent. In such very common cases, inquiry ordinarily reveals that there is indeed a neurotic mistake here. The mistake consists in supposing that the guilt felt by the neurotic has its ground in the conscious, relatively "innocent" wish. Such an "innocent" wish is in fact a cover-up for the unconscious, childish, and irrational wish, which does merit the guilt in question. Freud tells of a person who

> told me that the only thing that had kept him going at that time had been the consolation given him by his friend, who had always brushed his self reproaches aside on the ground that they were grossly exaggerated. Hearing this, I took the opportunity of giving him a first glance at the underlying principles of psychoanalytic therapy. When there is a *mésalliance,* I began, between an affect and its ideational content (in this instance, between the intensity of the self-reproach and the occasion for it), a layman will say that the affect is too great for the occasion—that it is exaggerated—and that consequently the inference following from the self-reproach (the inference, that is, that the patient is a criminal) is false. On the contrary, the [analytic] physician says: "No. The affect is justified. The sense of guilt is not in itself open to further criticism. But it belongs to another content, which is unknown (*unconscious*), and which requires to be looked for. The known ideational content has only got into its actual position owing to a false connection."[8]

It is perhaps because of this extremely common phenomenon that the casual observer or reader of case histories gets the impression that the guilt felt is disproportionate to the wish. The psychoanalyst in general assumes the guilt has a ground and looks further.

It is plausible to argue that there are at least some cases where the guilt is genuinely disproportionate. Typical of such cases is masturbation. Masturbation is the real cause of intense and widespread guilt-feeling. But contemporary science has changed our views on the topic. It can be reasonable to reduce such guilt by a change in the patient's moral standards, rather than by eliminating the wish.

Psychoanalytic inquiry reveals, however, that the major part of the guilt-feeling is often the fantasizing which accompanies the masturbation. It is the unconscious and conscious wishes and daydreams, which the act of masturbation helps to express, that evoke the guilt-feelings. These fantasies are likely to be incestuous, sadistic, masochistic, or in other ways prone to arouse guilt-feelings in many people in Western culture.

Here again we can see that the solution indicated is not a general "loosening up" of inner standards or conscience with respect to masturbation. Neither psychoanalyst nor moralist would argue that our taboos against incest, or possibly sadism, need to be eliminated. The ultimate solution is to modify or eliminate such wishes, not to give them moral approval.

Freud spoke in this context of the "omniscience of the super-ego." Prior to the existence of the superego in human beings, the sense of guilt corresponded with the actual carrying out of the violent deed. But in the course of the civilizing process, with the coming into existence of the superego, "a sense of guilt could be produced not only by an act of violence that is actually carried out, . . . but also by one that is merely intended (as psycho-analysis has discovered)."[9] In short, the wish becomes psychologically equivalent to the deed. It is clear that not only the content of my thesis but even the "moralistic" language in which it is cast is consistent with Freud's own usage.

Thus, irrational as it may seem to the twentieth-century enlightened mind, if psychoanalysis is taken seriously, it supports the position taken by many moral seers in both West and East.

It is essentially alien to the major objectives of psychoanalytic therapy to loosen conscience, weaken ideals, or reduce guilt by reminding the patient that he has not done what he unconsciously wished. Nor is it therapeutic to comment that everyone has such wishes, and that they can hardly be helped. If this latter approach were correct, then psychoanalysts would indeed merely "loosen" up the conscience. In fact, however, far from relaxing our justified moral judgments, success in psychoanalytic therapy results in helping us to become moral (and rational).

Yet we cannot ignore the fact that in therapy the psychoanalyst is not usually found calling these things morally evil. This absence of moralizing language and manner may give the impression that the therapist has a morally neutral attitude toward them. Psychoanalysis does not call for the puritanical rejection of persons having evil impulses, nor does the therapist condemn or demand abandonment of the patient's evil impulses. It is for the patient to face those impulses, find them wanting, and thereby change at her own initiative.

Another reason why we often overlook the fundamental implications of psychoanalytic therapy has to do with questions of technique rather than ultimate objectives. Frequently the objective of the therapist is to reduce guilt-feelings independently of removing the wish. But when this is so, it is a technical objective, with strictly limited and temporary scope during some special phase of psychoanalysis.

For example, if unconscious aggression against a parent moves toward consciousness, guilt-anxiety builds up and this serves to re-enforce the repression. However, if the therapist can enable the patient to feel less guilty, then the anxiety may become bearable. The result can be that the patient does consciously experience the wish, i.e., achieves insight. Experiencing the wish consciously enables the patient to engage in rational (ego) criticism of the guilty wish. Reduction of guilt feelings with this purpose in view is thus a temporary therapeutic technique, not a therapeutic or moral goal.

Surprisingly enough for those unacquainted with psychiatric theory and practice, one of the first phenomena to show itself in the patient's consciousness is the experiencing of the true depth of his guilt-feeling. For it is very frequently the case that the true depth and quality of the guilt is unconscious. Thus the first step often consists in making the person sharply aware of his profound guilt.

When the patient has thus faced his guilt, the next objective is to uncover the ground of the guilt. Where there is neurosis, the ground of the guilt will be unconscious, although a supposed ground may be present in consciousness. This supposed ground may be obviously inadequate for such guilt, or it may appear plausible. Still, analyst and patient must look behind it. Eventually the true motives that create the guilt become conscious. The struggle by the patient to hide, disguise, and repress these is ordinarily a long and painful one. If the problem is major, as in neurosis, the real guilty wish will be found to be deeply rooted in the patient's response to some fundamental human relationship. It is likely to be at the "core" of his personality.

There is an aspect of this process which deserves fuller description because it is psychologically and morally crucial and yet it is too often ignored or misunderstood in lay discussion. To become conscious of the wish is to experience oneself as wishing what is irrational or childish and a relic of the past. Hence, it is not a matter of being told about the wish or merely acknowledging it intellectually. The therapist may have a very good idea of what wishes are repressed, and could inform the patient. This is not insight.

At this stage of the process, the patient is at last able to reflect upon the wish in the context of his present life and maturity. Being able to appraise his wish realistically, he at last is able to reject the wish, to modify it, or—if it still seems viable—to live it consciously. It is no longer a matter of uncontrollable, irrational reactions.

Such a restructuring or rejection of a deep-rooted wish is not easy. It requires on the part of the patient much energy. It calls for a combination of rational deliberation, experience-testing, and bearing with anxiety while moving toward new goals. It can be as difficult to create a constructive solution as it has been to discover the previous inadequate solution. At least it is done without the self-defeating tension that burdened the patient when under the full sway of his neurosis.

A deeply rooted wish is likely to have certain features that cannot be eradicated. There is no way to completely undo sexuality, aggressiveness, or other biologically rooted impulses. Nor is it likely that a person will become entirely free of those basic modes of response learned in earliest years and that color all subsequent learning. Nor are fundamental cultural responses likely to be radically abandoned. All of these, however, can be significantly modified, and often in a wide variety of ways.

The most fundamental and enduring modification is likely to be what psychoanalysis calls sublimation and drive-neutralization. This retains the generic features of the wish. However there is a substantial modification of the specific quality and aim of the wish to make it more rational and harmonious with the mature personality. A typical example of such sublimations is the transformation of infantile homosexual motives into brotherly, humanitarian love and various forms of friendship.

There are interesting cases which may at times appear to be exceptions to the general principles mentioned here. For example, it is possible to feign guilt-feeling as a disguise for some other feeling. In such cases the "guilt-feeling" may simply disappear with insight. Or again, it is possible to identify oneself with someone (consciously or unconsciously) and as a consequence of this identification one also feels the guilt of that person. In this latter case, the guilt may be eradicated, along with the wish, by undoing the identification.

We are now prepared to develop more fully the moral implications of the previous discussions. I begin by presenting some excerpts from a contemporary and exceedingly clear exposition of the kind of philosophic interpretation of psychoanalysis that I hold to be wrong. In this way we can set off most sharply the correct perspective on moral responsibility as seen from a psychoanalytic standpoint.

> In a deeper sense we cannot hold the person responsible: we can hold his neurosis responsible, but *he is not responsible for his neurosis,* particularly since the age at which its onset was inevitable was an age before he could even speak.[10]

Hospers, the writer of the above, says further, "Between an unconscious that willy-nilly determined your actions, and an external force which pushes you, there is little if anything to choose. The unconscious is just *as if* it were an outside force. . . ."[11]

Hospers presents a deductive argument to support his position. During the course of it, he makes two assumptions of a moral nature. He assumes (1) that we cannot be held responsible for an event over which we have no control. One such event, he says, is the neurosis we acquire in childhood. He further assumes (2) that we cannot be held responsible for anything that happens as an inevitable result of an uncontrollable event. It follows that we cannot be held responsible as adults for actions that stem from our adult neuroses. This formulation of the psychoanalytic hypotheses is debatable, but his version provides us with what ought to be the most difficult form of the argument with which to deal.

Granting his assumptions, Hospers's argument seems plausible. But what can we make of it in the light of our analysis of psychoanalysis in the preceding sections of this essay?

We have seen that the essence of therapeutic and moral progress is to experience and acknowledge oneself as actually wishing the guilty wish. It is also to perceive the neurotic behavior as one's truly willed action. This is in effect to accept responsibility. It is to accept as ours the task of doing something about these wishes or consciously suffering the moral and psychological consequences. Thus Hospers assumed that we cannot be held responsible for the inevitable consequence of uncontrollable events. Yet we see that in therapy an acceptance of responsibility is a necessary and distinctive outcome.

As do so many moralists, Hospers looks to the antecedents of the act in order to settle responsibility. The real issue as revealed by our present perspective is otherwise. As a moral agent I must accept responsibility as the person I am now and go on from here. As an adult who is able in some measure to control what happens, I must face myself as I am, not picking and choosing. I must endeavor to act as now seems reasonable to me in light of my maturity. The neurotic, who is unconscious of the true problem, typically cannot do this without the preliminary aid of therapy.

The temptation is to ask: "But why should I accept responsibility for that which I could not help?" The implication of this rhetorical question is that this is an unjustifiable burden. And it will always appear unjustifiable so long as one looks to the past for the reason. It is to the future, however, that we must look for the justification of this profound moral demand. It is not that we were children and thus nonresponsible but rather that we are aiming to become mature persons. This ideal, and not the past, is the ground for the demand that we accept responsibility for what we are. This is so even though we are in many ways morally flawed and even though we cannot change the past.

Guilt is retrospective; responsibility is prospective. Guilt is for what was wished or done. Responsibility is for what shall be done.

The matter is as simple and direct as in the case of a natural disaster. I am a member of the community. I face the disaster and say, "I had no control over what happened." (Indeed, I am in this instance guilty for none of it.) Nevertheless, I accept responsibility; I will clean up and help repair this area. What else can I do except cry, "I couldn't help it!"

It is only in a derivative sense that we are responsible for what has happened in the past. The common emphasis upon responsibility as pertaining to things past is understandable from a practical stand-point, but it has obscured the essentials of the matter. Being responsible for what has happened implies that one accepted responsibility, tacitly or explicitly, in the doing of it. Thus we do not judge a person to be responsible for what he has done until he has reached an appropriate age of responsibility. This in turn is presumptive evidence that he accepts responsibility in cases where it is normally accepted. Public announcement of such acceptance is, of course, not necessary, in fact not typical. If the person's behavior shows no confirming signs of such acceptance of responsibility, we treat him as nonresponsible, a moral child. In clear-cut cases, we provide a guardian.

When a person is in need of psychotherapy, it is implicit that she had in fact not accepted responsibility in certain areas of her life. Hence we allow her claim to therapy rather than moral judgment. In successful psychoanalytic therapy, the patient at last becomes responsible. She achieves autonomy by her acceptance of responsibility, and she takes on the burdens of being held responsible.

It takes humility to accept responsibility. To say, as criticism, that this is not "fair" or "just" is to suppose that the world is fair and just—which is precisely what the world is not.

Irrelevant to the present discussion are such metaphysical issues as determinism and indeterminism. Whether the accepting of responsibility is "inevitable," "caused," or "free," it is a fact that accepting responsibility is a necessary condition of maturity. Those who do not, or "cannot" do so, for whatever reason, are in fact doomed never to have psychological and moral integrity.

It is possible at this point to see how, in a passage previously cited, Hospers is correct in his facts but incorrect in his interpretation. He suggests that the unconscious, insofar as it is uncontrollable, is alien to us. The purport of psychoanalytic therapy, however, is that we must come to acknowledge the unconscious as part of the self, not as alien to it. We learn from psychoanalysis that to treat the unconscious as alien to the self, in the morally significant sense, is to subvert the self. It is to remove an important part of oneself from rational control. It is a surrender of integrity.

The liberating attitude consists in acknowledging the unconscious as morally integral to oneself, undertaking the ordeal of facing openly what was unconscious, and then dealing with these now conscious infantile impulses in the light of one's mature appreciation of the issues.

Orestes' Task

The Story of Orestes

Oedipus killed his father. Orestes kills his mother. For psychoanalysts, the Oedipus complex has been central. Yet it is the story of Orestes that has served as a main plot for such writers as O'Neill, Eliot, and Sartre.

There are a few psychoanalytic or quasi-psychoanalytic discussions of Orestes.[1] For the most part they present his story as a "homosexual" variant on the Oedipus story. Though interesting points have been made in these discussions, a principal psychological significance of the story has been missed. The key to understanding the psychological significance of the Orestes story is to see it as the continuation of the Oedipal motif.

The Oedipus story is familiar, but the story of Orestes bears telling. The story is brief and bloody. King Agamemnon, Orestes' father, returns from the Trojan wars after ten years. He is unaware that his wife, Queen Clytemnestra, has been ruling along with her paramour, Aegisthus. Agamemnon is trapped by the two lovers and murdered. Orestes comes home, shattered by what has happened. He recognizes his duty to avenge his father's murder. Agonizing though it is for him, he confronts his mother. She abandons pretense and begs

This is a revised version of a previously published essay: "Orestes: Paradigm Hero and Central Motif of Contemporary Ego Psychology," fiftieth anniversary issue, *Psychoanalytic Review* (Fall 1963): 87–111.

for the mercy due a mother. Orestes wavers. But he does what must be done. He kills her and Aegisthus.

The Oedipus story crystallized Freud's early great insights into the development of the instinctual drives. I believe that the Orestes story crystallizes in mythic form Freud's later insights about the role of the ego and superego. The Orestes story forms a framework within which the new ego psychology is organically related to the earlier Oedipal insights. It portrays the movement into adult responsibility.

In the analysis presented here I do not claim to give the "real" meaning of the Orestes story. Nor am I engaged in a treasure hunt for choice psychoanalytic "symbols." Great mythic drama such as Aeschylus's *Oresteia* has profundity, richness, and perennial powers of illumination. In so saying, I mean that the *Oresteia* does not have one meaning, but many. Explications of a meaning, such as the one I shall give, are to be tested by reference to this dramatic unity of many meanings.

The specific text that guides me in the following is Aeschylus's trilogy, the *Oresteia,* taken with due regard for its setting, and with special reference to Orestes himself.[2]

Oedipal Conflict and Orestean Resolution

We must begin with some very brief remarks about the story of Oedipus the King. It is, psychologically, the essential background for the Orestes story. As will be recalled, Oedipus has a fate announced by the oracles: he is to kill his father and marry his mother. This prophecy becomes a reality, although Oedipus is unaware of the significance of his actions. Later, upon seeing the true nature and horror of his deeds, he tears out his eyes and takes himself into exile.

This story reflects the psychic pattern that was one of Freud's earliest and greatest discoveries. The male infant is destined to achieve his first genuine psychic unity at a phase of his life when he is dominated by erotic impulses toward his mother and destructive impulses toward his "rival," that is, his father. This is all a matter of unconscious fantasy. In actuality, the psychic relationships are far more complex than this first simple formula suggests. The whole complex pattern constitutes the Oedipal conflict—a pattern with as many individual variants as there are individual human beings.

This Oedipal conflict is the "fate" of the male child; yet, as in the Sophocles play, it is a fate that is not something "externally" imposed, nor is it magic or miracle. In the play and in life, it is simply the fate that the individual himself brings about by his own actions, actions that then have their natural consequences. To be told of this "fate" is ineffectual, mere words. Each male must live the Oedipal situation. But frustrated erotic love of the mother and aggressive but fearful rivalry with the father is a dead end.

Here is where the psychological content of the Orestes story merges with that of Oedipus's story. Oedipus and Orestes represent, psychologically, one individual: Oedipus is the individual as he moves into the central growth dilemma and crisis; Orestes is the individual as he successfully moves out of it. Orestes exhibits human liberation from the Oedipal dilemma. There is no doubt that the overall theme of the *Oresteia* is one of salvation, harmony, and liberation.

We leave Oedipus as one who exiles himself in horror from the scene of his crime. Orestes, the young man, is introduced on stage as returning from exile to his royal home, and discovering the murder of his father and a quasi-incestuous liaison of his mother with Aegisthus. The latter is in effect a stand-in for the Oedipus who killed the father in order to marry the mother.

Oedipus was fated to do as he did. So, too, is the young boy in entering the Oedipal conflict situation. Orestes, however, does not have a fate, but a destiny. The difference is vital. Orestes becomes conscious of the situation and acts deliberately to do what he sees as his duty. He is, after all, the son and heir of the house of Atreus, and he must take up the responsibilities of this role. He could, if he chose, remain an exile. However, Apollo's oracle told him that if he did not take up his responsibility, he would suffer from decay of spirit, sickness of body, and the rejection of men. But in the *Oresteia* it is quite clear that Orestes can refuse to accept this responsibility.

It is of interest to notice the psychological dynamics that the Orestes story expresses. It reflects the repression of the Oedipal impulses in several ways. In the play, the crimes that Orestes learns about are not his doing. This corresponds to the repression of the Oedipal attachments. So, too, does the fact that in the play the crimes occurred in the past. Likewise, Aegisthus, who has aided in the murder of Agamemnon and married his wife, is a nephew of Clytemnestra, thus making the marriage incestuous.

Here it is obvious that Aegisthus is a stand-in for Oedipus. Orestes, in turn, represents a new stage in the development of the play and in the psychological maturation process. In this way, the older Oedipal role of the son is projected onto a suitable substitute. Orestes represents the new persona.

The conscious feelings of Orestes as he deliberates upon the situation are precisely what the psychological analysis would lead us to expect. Orestes feels repugnance toward Aegisthus, the Oedipal self to be destroyed. He now feels reverence and love tinged with awe of the father, once his rival, now to be his spiritual ally. In a ceremony, Orestes offers up a prayer to his father in which it is clear that he is now allying himself with his father. He prays: "I call on my dead father to hear, to sanction. . . . Now I am a man."[3]

Freud says, "the repression of the Oedipus complex was no easy task. . . . [The child's ego] borrowed strength to do this, so to speak, from the father, and this loan was an extraordinarily momentous event."[4]

These motives correspond to those that move the young male in the course of resolving the Oedipal conflict and reaching a fundamentally new psychic status. He must not only identify with the father, but also, as main tasks: (a) he must eliminate the image of the mother as object of erotic and illicit love, thus freeing himself for non-incestuous and noncompetitive love attachments; (b) he must break free from his infantile dependence on the mother, thus decisively establishing his own autonomy and his own maleness; (c) by doing these things, he eliminates the fantasies of himself in the role of mother's consort and father's usurper. In the play, and in the traditional story, the point is made more bluntly: Orestes kills his mother and Aegisthus.

Does Orestes not feel morally conflicted about these killings? Is there no psychic conflict in the young male? The answer is not simple. The killing of Aegisthus presents no conflict to Orestes. "*His* death gets no word from me," says Orestes curtly. This corresponds to the psychological point that the childish self is now looked on with scorn. The killing of Clytemnestra, however, poses a more formidable problem. She is, after all, Orestes' own mother. She bore him, nursed him— and, for a while, no doubt she loved and was loved by him. She is a strong woman, manlike in her force of will and mind. When Orestes has at last slain Aegisthus, Clytemnestra rushes upon the scene.

At this juncture, for the first and only time during the play, Orestes genuinely hesitates. "Pylades!" he cries out to the hitherto silent companion of his travels—"Pylades, what shall I do? To kill a mother is terrible. Shall I show mercy?"[5]

Pylades, who by name, origin, and function in the play represents Apollo, now utters the only lines he has in the play. They are few, but decisive: "Where then are Apollo's words, his Pythian oracles? What become of men's sworn oaths? Make all men living your enemies, but not the gods."[6]

This is the moment, then, when the most awe-ful and shocking of crimes is to be committed out of a moral and spiritual necessity. Of course, Orestes already has weighty reasons for doing what he is about to do; of course, he knows that he has previously bound himself to do it in sacred oath. He knows what he must do, and yet—"to kill a mother is terrible."[7]

What is needed in such momentous action is support from the very deepest sources of strength, sources that transcend the realm of the voluntary, the conscious, the planned. Nothing but the very voice of the divine will swing the balance. Here, too, a profound psychological truth is expressed: This, says Freud, is a "struggle which [rages] in the deepest strata of the mind."[8] And as to these deepest sources of the youth's masculinity, our knowledge of it is "something ultimate . . . [it is a problem] which clearly falls wholly within the province of biology."[9]

In both the Orestes myth and the psychoanalytical formulation, the decisive forces at the critical moment transcend the conscious and voluntary. They surge out of the depths (or heights) that activate us but that are not controlled by us.

Yet we do not deal here with a complete subjection to forces beyond us. The decisive balance of psychological forces is not, for Freud, merely a matter of biology. He speaks again and again in terms of struggle, will, mastery. The ego must "properly master the Oedipus complex." Or again, more plainly, in speaking of the therapy of the neurotic (who, after all, is belatedly dealing with these same problems), Freud says that the neurotic "must find the courage to direct his attention to the phenomena of his illness. His illness itself must no longer seem to him contemptible, but must become an enemy worthy of his mettle. . . ."[10]

Freud assures us that when we are seeing the Oedipus Rex of Sophocles' play, we respond unconsciously to the guilt in our own Oedipal self: "You are struggling in vain against your responsibility. . . . [you are] bound to be aware of this responsibility as a sense of guilt whose basis is unknown to [you]."[11]

How can the deed be one in which the individual accepts responsibility, is responsible, and yet is moved by forces that transcend his control? The question is fundamental, and the answer is at best complex when not entirely shrouded in mystery. But the task of clarification is not one we need take up here. The point is that the paradox holds equally in the psychoanalytic account of the matter and in the *Oresteia*. Furthermore, it is a distinctive paradox. It is central to every doctrine in which personal responsibility dwells side by side with the operation of forces transcending the conscious will. The Orestes story brings out the paradox sharply, and thus it frames for us a central paradox in the psychology of the individual's "coming of age" as well as in the notion of responsibility itself.

Freud summarizes what I would call the Orestean task in the following words:

> the human individual has to devote himself to the great task of detaching himself from his parents; and not until that task is achieved can he cease to be a child and become a member of the social community. For the son, this task consists in detaching his libidinal wishes from his mother, and employing them for the choice of a real outside love-object, and in reconciling himself with his father if he has remained in opposition to him. . . .[12]

In analyzing the exile, torment, and purification that actually do follow the Orestean deed, we must recall that, psychologically, this is never accomplished in one stroke. The child learns to join the "social community" as a social being, learns necessary social skills, schools its intellect.[13] The child, in short, wanders through the outer world, as does Orestes after his murders. He is an exile, "long wandering through tribes and towns . . . welcoming homes." He meets new "friends whose homes and hands have given me welcome without harm or taint."[14]

The second great stage of Oedipal conflict and its Orestean resolution is the stormy period of adolescence. At this time, the old instinctual drives take on a new force. The son must deepen anew the identification with the father, put away decisively the tempting and dominating mother, become his father's heir rather than his rival, and seek an independent life in the world. And Freud stressed that until the ego has "properly mastered the Oedipus complex,"[15] the residue of the old conflict will also involve the tension between ego and superego that is moral "impurity," or guilt.[16]

Perhaps we should note here that in the Aeschylean trilogy, Apollo, Orestes' "sponsor," is explicitly and emphatically identified as the representative of the new, male-oriented generation of gods.

This long period required to translate repression into sublimation may in everyday life be a battle fought again and again. In the *Oresteia* we see it as a single, long exile devoted to self-purification and to communal acceptance.

It seems appropriate now to amplify a statement offered at the outset of this study. I believe it is due to the relatively late formulation and discussion of Freud's theses on ego psychology that such an early play as O'Neill's *Mourning Becomes Electra* treats the Orestes story primarily in terms of Oedipal conflict. Eliot has seen beyond this, as has Sartre, though the one takes a religious and the other an atheistic stand.

Our view of the Orestes story provides us with a further and quite specific perspective upon a central contemporary predicament. Aeschylus's Orestes leaves for Argos, where he will carry on the family line and take up his royal role. By contrast, Sartre's Orestes, after having committed the killings, abandons Argos and is left wandering in exile, pursued by the Furies. The Greek Orestes had his established role as heir to the throne, once free. Sartre's Orestes has only freedom. His anguish is just beginning, for now he knows he is free and must create an identity for himself, a world to inhabit. But he must create it out of nothing. The contemporary emphasis on the "quest for identity" in psychological literature takes its place in the Orestes story exactly as it should.

In our culture, unlike that of ancient Greece, we are conscious of all cultures. Therefore the psychological task of creating an identity may have no general solution so far as content goes. The existentialists have insisted that this is what it is to be genuinely free.

Yet it may be that we overestimate our freedom with regard to the range of choices we have, the possibilities of new creation.

Perhaps we are more like Orestes than we think. Our archaic family ties, our subjugation to the dwellers in the dark caverns of the mind may all be more unyielding than we would acknowledge. These may hold us to our individual fate or destiny the more urgently for being unacknowledged.

Retributive Punishment

What if the captain gave the sergeant a legitimate command, the sergeant did not obey the command, and the captain did nothing about it? Doesn't the captain *have* to punish the sergeant? Why?

Deserved punishment is called retribution. Retribution has been characterized as an unenlightened practice, a variant of vengeance.[1] Although there have been modern defenders of retributive punishment for crime, the preponderant opinion, at least among the more intellectually and morally sophisticated, has been that retribution is a vestigial motivation that, however popular it may be among the general public, ought ideally to be rejected.[2]

By the hypothesis, nothing is intended to be accomplished by a purely retributive punishment except the result that the law-breaker suffers. The purported reason or purpose is to impose what the law-breaker deserves, but we cannot explain what "deserves" means. Why should we make someone suffer because of something that is already done and over?

In an earlier essay on retributive punishment under law I argued that a policy of retributive punishment is a necessity, not an option.[3] Here I want to restate the thesis and generalize it to all forms of command. Further, I want to argue for proportionality. In other words, I want to show that in any retributive system of punishment, the punishment necessarily "fits" the crime.

This is a substantially revised version of "Punishment and Suffering" (Presidential address, American Philosophical Association, 1977).

To put this view into perspective, and then to explain and justify it, we can begin with at least brief consideration of some extant theories of punishment.

Brief Review of Past Theories

In one form or another, it has been held by many commentators that punishment—and in particular punishment for law breaking—is retribution for wrongdoing. While "wrongdoing" may be used in the context of the law as synonymous with "lawbreaking," commonly the implication intended in philosophical discussions of punishment is a moral one. "Wrongdoing" is used to mean doing what is morally wrong. Kant saw punishment for crime as an absolute moral imperative.[4] There are many variations of this morality-oriented view of punishment for lawbreaking[5]; for instance, Michael Moore has argued a modern version of the view that the criminal "deserves" to be punished.

On the other hand, writers such as Mabbott are emphatic in declaring that retributive punishment for lawbreaking is an obligation deriving from the punitive provisions of the law and the judge's pledge to execute the law.[6]

Still a third approach, typically overlapping with the moral approach, consists in seeing punishment as retributive in that it restores a certain equilibrium. Morris, for example, writes that the criminal, by his unlawful act, has an "unfair advantage" over law-abiding citizens. The punishment is then viewed as a deprivation that "erases" this unfair advantage. A familiar image of this is that the criminal "pays" for the crime in being punished.

Each of these types of views poses familiar and, I think, insoluble difficulties. For example, the notion that punishment under law is the criminal's just desert for doing wrong depends in part on the tacit presumption that it is always morally wrong to violate a law. Yet we know that inevitably some laws are ill-conceived and obedience amounts to doing what is morally wrong. Hence, insofar as conduct amounts to disobedience of such a law, the conduct is not morally wrong, and yet under the law it would be punishable. If one holds that such a morally justified violation is not truly punishable, one makes the moral doctrine internally consistent, but this still begs the question whether punishment is necessarily for moral wrongs only.

The thesis that the law prescribes punishment, and the judge is pledged to execute the law faithfully, tells us nothing of substance about the reason for prescribing punishment in the first place. The basic question is not why the judge imposes punishment on the criminal, but why punishment is an appropriate response to crime and therefore warrants being the response adopted in law.

It is a puzzling notion that punishment erases the unfair advantage, or is payment for the crime. Such ideas amount to metaphors that need explanation. Certainly the criminal conduct itself is not literally undone, nor is the harm it causes transformed into no harm. For some types of crimes the harm can be "undone" in a metaphorical sense by requiring the criminal to pay back—literally pay with money—the money illegally taken. This monetary restitution is a kind of "paying for the crime." Yet at best this is true only insofar as the criminal harm consisted of a specific monetary loss.

Indeed even with a payback, the fact remains that the original deed was a crime. If the command to pay back the money, even with interest, were the total response of the law, then in effect the theft would amount to a legal form of involuntary loan. That is, it would be legally acceptable to take money at will, and without consent of the owner, so long as one eventually paid it back. Such is certainly not the intent of the law against theft.

Moreover it is only certain types of crimes where monetary payment in some intelligible sense negates or "erases" the harm. Paying damages for having caused the loss of a limb, destroyed a unique natural habitat, or irreparably slashed a Rembrandt cannot be viewed as undoing the harm. Nor can monetary payment repay or negate the crime of rape.

Nor for that matter is it clear what is meant, and why it is justified, to say that punishment is a criminal's "just desert." Absent further explanation, this amounts to no more than a restatement as dogma that criminals ought to be punished. It is a dogma because no reason or argument is provided.

The Necessity for Retribution

Imagine that a valid law is passed prohibiting a certain kind of conduct. Those who may contemplate engaging in such conduct consider what consequences follow if they defy this law. To their surprise they discover that there is no intent to punish violators, no policy for retribution of any kind for engaging in the conduct. What conclusions can reasonably be drawn?

Prospective lawbreakers see the law as a toothless tiger. It says you must not do it, but it also says, at least implicitly, that you will not suffer at the hands of the law if you do choose to do it. The "prohibition" may have persuasive or suggestive force. Or it may have the practical force of a request, or an expression of the desires of the lawmakers. But having said you should not do it, the lawmakers wash their hands of the matter so far as making you suffer as the result of doing it. They have had their say, and as far as they are concerned that is the end of the matter.

What is true of the law's commands and their penalty-conditions is true generally, *mutatis mutandis*, of commands in general. When the captain gave an authorized command to the sergeant, there had to be an implicit intent to punish disobedience. Without an understanding that there is a realistic intent to punish disobedience, the "command" would not be a command. The sergeant would see through the form and manner of the captain's words, and would take the directive as the captain's way of forcefully expressing a desire or a suggestion.

Essentially the same holds true of an organizational regulation, a parent's orders to the child, or the rules of sport. Where there is no policy for penalty, it is understood that what is desired is not actually required. Even the child learns to recognize those parental "commands" that are no more than forceful expressions of what is desired, and distinguishes these from parental orders when the parent "really means it."

A system of legislative pronouncements unsupported by a policy of punishing infractions would not be a system of *law* as we understand the term. It would be a system of official proposals so far as it played any directive role in the life of the citizenry. The language of command would be a kind of hyperbole.

The general principles underlying the relation of law and punishment are as follows.

We should begin by distinguishing between the various forms of command and the various forms of proposals. By "command" I mean such things as orders, commands, laws, requirements, rules, and regulations. By "proposals" I mean such things as suggestions, advice, requests, and pleas. Commands are distinguished by their imperative force. If not complied with, they have failed to be effective as commands. Proposals are in contrast not imperative. They propose a line of action, but do not require that it be adopted. If not adopted, they still may be effective as proposals provided they have been given reasonable consideration prior to action.

The question we can usefully ask here is: what must be the case if a directive is to be a command that is effective? Consider, for example, what must be true of an effective law. Here we have to appreciate the paradoxical way in which a law governs our will. Given a law to which I am subject, it must be the case that I have the power to will to comply or to will to act in violation of the law. In short, the law leaves my will free in this regard. Nevertheless, the law has power over my will (if it is law that is effective), and it governs my will. The law has power over my will in that I either will to respect its provisions or else, upon my failing to do so, the law subsequently imposes a frustration of my will. Punishment, the imposition of suffering, is a frustration of my will.

The freedom of choice that I have under law is thus of a large but still limited kind. In any situation there usually are many possible lawful ways for me to act. I can express myself, act creatively and imaginatively, or follow custom and habit. All these options are open to me except for one: I must bend before the law. That is to say, if of my own free will I choose not to comply, that is the sufficient condition for the law to make me suffer, thereby frustrating my offending will.

It follows that if I have the *power* to act without respect for law, and if no legal constraints on my will follow as consequence, then so far as the law is concerned my will is unqualifiedly *un*constrained by law. This amounts to saying that I am *completely* free to do as I wish. In truth, whatever the legal language, it does not truly require me to act in any specific way. It is not law in force.

One obvious qualification of the above is in order. The agents of the law do not always succeed in finding, convicting, and punishing those who have violated the law. Like all institutions, the legal system is fallible. What is essential is that there be a realistic policy of punishing violators, even if execution of the policy is imperfect.

Likewise it is a practical necessity that those subject to the law generally do will to act conformably to that law. They may do so out of respect for law, for other reasons, or for a mixture of reasons. But conformity to law must in any case be an overriding consideration where motives to act in ways contrary to law exist. Either those subject to law generally do conform to law, or the legal system is ipso facto a failure.

The gist of the preceding remarks can be expressed as follows: What distinguishes commands from proposals is the association of a penalty-condition with commands, and the absence of such a condition in the case of proposals. When we advise, suggest, recommend, request, we do not intend any penalty-condition for failure to comply. When we command, order, rule, demand, we do intend a penalty-condition, and we intend the subject of the command to be aware of this.

Proposals have their fulfillment if the proposal is given due consideration, even if not accepted. Commands are fulfilled only if there is either obedience or punishment for disobedience.

None of the preceding is intended to rule out objectives such as deterrence, reform, or social benefit when dealing with disobedience. Any of these objectives may be reasonable, provided that they coincide with the retributive penalty-condition.

What are we to make in this context of the commands of morality? I speak of these as commands here, and thereby exclude utilitarian theories of morality. On utilitarian theories, an act is morally right by reason of the beneficial consequences. Utilitarian moral directives become, at most, an informative recommendation.

If we seek to understand "moral law" as more than a metaphor, as a genuine form of command upon us, it can be helpful to turn to the inward looking and love-oriented teaching of Jesus. The Old Testament buttressed the law with Divine punishment or the human lex talionis. In contrast, Jesus said, "Love God, and love thy neighbor as thyself."

I take it that this teaching does not mean we should love our neighbor as much as we do ourselves. Instead it means we should love our neighbor as if that neighbor *were* ourselves. It proposes identification with the other. Thus, in doing moral injury to another, I am doing moral injury to myself.

At least from this Christian standpoint the moral command is a genuine form of command upon us, for it does have a penalty-condition. It is the guilt we suffer, the spiritual pain we impose on ourselves for the wrong we have done to ourselves. This is retribution for our failure to comply with moral commands we make upon ourselves. That guilt is what demonstrates the authenticity of the moral commands we make on ourselves. No external source of retribution is necessary.

There are many who cannot appreciate the force of internal moral command. They require an external wielder of a penalty-condition for breaches of morality. Here we encounter the Old Testament attitude, an attitude to be found in other traditions, too. Breaches of morality are breaches of God's command, and as such will be punished by God. This view is more concrete, more readily explained and understood than the view of morality as that which is intrinsically right, and perceived as such by the moral sensibility. The "external" view of morality's penalty-condition accounts for a widespread popular belief that atheists cannot be given moral trust.

As the preceding remarks about the commands of morality suggest, the essential point can be stated independently of theistic teachings. All we need to assume is that the moral sensibility suffices to confront one with demands one makes upon oneself and that call upon one's self-respect. Violation of what we genuinely perceive as the right is therefore necessarily to experience guilt and loss of self-respect. Indeed the failure to feel guilt or loss of self-respect is sure evidence that one did not genuinely see the act as wrong.

A question that inevitably arises concerns the deterrent effect of a policy of punishment. Isn't deterrence the real aim of punishment for crime? Certainly there is no question that the penalty-condition does have a deterrent role. An effective penalty-condition must be something that the person to whom the command is addressed would prefer to avoid, and thus is a deterrent.

Given that a penalty-condition is the distinctive and essential feature of a command as distinguished from a request, and given also that a penalty-condition must be a deterrent, it may seem that a retributive punishment regime is in fact a deterrent regime. This is not the case, however.

If deterrence were a fundamental aim, then retribution would be optional rather than necessary. For in some types of cases, or perhaps in all, deterrence might be better achieved by education or psychotherapy, aroused public attitudes, enhanced organizational structures, or manipulation of the physical environment to discourage or prevent lawbreaking. Retribution would then be merely one species of deterrence, and therefore optional. Yet this conclusion cannot be accepted.

Although the penalty-condition essential to retribution must be a deterrent, the fundamental aim of a true retributive system is to establish laws as meaningful commands. It is the integrity of the command that is validated by retributive punishment. This is a necessity regardless of whether there are other and more effective deterrents available in the particular case.

Retribution is backward-looking. Deterrence on the other hand is directed to the prevention of future acts of violation.

Proportionality

A penalty-condition applies as a result of disobedience to a command. Since the penalty-condition is the command-specific response to the disobedience, it necessarily reflects the way the commander views the significance of that disobedience.

One need not know the specific pragmatic considerations or moral views of a community to know the relative gravity they assign to various violations of law. One need only know the punishment assigned to violation of a particular law as compared to violations of others.

Were a ruthless dictator to decree that any disobedience to his personal commands was punishable by death, we would know, regardless of the specific nature of the act, that disobedience to his commands was the capital crime that took priority.

It is not merely that it is the custom to assign proportionate punishments nor does it matter what the one who makes the command says about the gravity of disobedience. The punishment for disobedience is what tells the tale so far as the force of the command is concerned. A light sentence for what is labeled a grave crime sends the true message, the message that the crime is viewed lightly.

Let us imagine that robbery merited a ten-dollar fine, and over-parking a hundred-dollar fine. Under such circumstances we would have only two options: Either we would have to conclude that (for reasons we fail to see) the authorities view over-parking as a much graver delinquency than robbery. Or else we would have to conclude that this punishment policy is irrational. It embodies no system of punishment, and leaves the punishment as the arbitrary, ad hoc choice of the punisher.

This intuitive judgment emerges because we expect the retributive aspect of punishment to be the limiting condition with which the other responses to crime must be compatible. If we assign a lesser punishment to an act of disobedience, we cannot rationally claim it nevertheless remains as grave as before.

How are penalty-conditions determined? The direct and general answer is that the system of penalty-conditions is determined by the commander, in any way the commander chooses, with whatever purposes the commander chooses to adopt. This is a conceptual point, not a practical one. In practice, as is obvious, any particular command authority will be constrained by a variety of considerations: moral, legal, political, traditional, social, pragmatic, or even vengeful. It is not that the measure of punishment need be selected on rational grounds. Rather it is that, given a scale of punishments, the authority setting that scale necessarily reveals thereby its true view of the relative gravity of the commands to which the scale applies.

Thus the measure chosen may be time of confinement, with five years as the maximum and thirty days as a minimum. Or it may be time of confinement with life as the maximum and one year as the minimum. It is the interval that necessarily measures the perceived gravity of the offense.

It is evident from even the briefest historical or multicultural study that the variations in penalty-condition patterns or scales is wide. It is possible to have different sets of penalty-conditions for different groups within a society, such as the conquered vis-à-vis the nobility or the slaves vis-à-vis the slave owners. Contemporary Western systems of justice have moved to a democratic, egalitarian pattern of penalty-conditions in which, at least ideally and to a large extent in practice, a single pattern of penalty-conditions holds for all individuals. For rational adults, only the nature of the offense is relevant to imposing a penalty-condition. The only relevant personal characteristics are immaturity or mental disability.

The further practical constraints in contemporary Western egalitarian practice are, broadly, moral acceptability and efficiency of administration. The moral considerations have very largely ruled out bodily mutilation, or punitively motivated bodily violence of any kind (with the exception of the death penalty in the U.S.). Considerations of deterrence, reform, and public symbolism are also common considerations.

Thus, for example, a superimposed five-year imprisonment for using a gun in the commission of a crime may seem to satisfy a variety of socially acceptable motives. Nevertheless two fundamental principles remain. There must be some punishment imposed if the law prohibiting the crime is to be effectively in force, and the addition of five years necessarily establishes that the use of a gun is considered by the legislature to increase the gravity of the crime. Indeed, the gravity of wielding the gun, as judged by those who set the sentence guidelines, is revealed by the location of the five-year punishment on the scale of all punishments.

Complicating matters, but not fundamentally changing them, are the variations in response to crime in which the offender is offered a choice. For example, in the case of a first offense of a drunken driver or drug abuser, the convicted individual may be given the alternatives of successfully completing a rehabilitation program or a specified period of imprisonment.

This tells us that it is not so grave an offense if the offender is willing to reform. In this case the law shows a certain degree of compassion and recognition of human frailty. On the other hand, confinement for the same offense by someone who chooses not to reform reflects a much graver crime because of its ominous potential.

Responsibility and Punishment

It has been held that punishment for an offense is not only what the offender deserves but what the rational offender desires. There is an important insight here, although it appears to be an unrealistic view.

I have argued that it is necessary that every command must have a penalty-condition. What I have tacitly presumed is that a command in force is addressed to a suitable subject. Here "suitable" means a responsible agent with respect to what is commanded. Plainly it makes no sense to punish someone for disobeying a command if that person does not have the capacity to respond to such a command. The incapacity may be physical, or it may be mental. But it only makes sense to command those who do have suitable capacity to respond.

Moreover, to be a responsible agent is perforce to be a suitable subject of commands. For example, to be a responsible soldier is to be a suitable subject of the commands of a superior officer. To be a responsible attorney is to be a suitable subject of appropriate commands of one's client and of the court. Thus, in general, to be a responsible person is to be a suitable subject of legitimate commands.

Since retributive punishment is an inherent feature of commands, punishment for disobedience is fulfillment of the command. Therefore punishment for disobedience evidences respect for one's having acted as a responsible agent. On the other hand, to choose not to punish (as in the case of those found to have been insane) amounts to treating the person as not responsible.

Hence the rational agent who understands the logic of retributive punishment would want to be recognized and treated as a responsible person. That, in turn, is to say that such a person would desire the punishment, even though it entails suffering. In short, the suffering is the price of responsibility.[7]

Conclusion

Thus in sum, a policy of retribution, that is, a policy of imposing a penalty-condition and proportionality of punishment, is a necessary feature of commands. This is true not only in law but in all commands generally as well.

Here I use "command" to mean what I have called a command in force, that is, a directive that actually functions in practice as a command. I distinguish commands in force from mere words or gestures that have the form and style of commands without evidence of a policy of retribution for failure to comply.

The response to disobedience to a command may be shaped by many motives, but the one motive that takes priority and that is always necessary is the motive of retribution by means of a penalty proportionate to the gravity of the offense. Only when a proportionate penalty is imposed can other responses, compatible with that penalty, be justified.

It deserves emphasis that a suitably proportionate penalty is not something determined entirely by the nature of the offense. It also reflects in a crucial way the commander's perception of the gravity of the offense relative to other types of offenses. The scale of punishments is not a measure of the gravity of the offense as somehow independently and objectively appraised. Instead it is the location on the scale assigned to the offense that reveals its gravity in the eyes of the punishment authority.

5

Alcoholism and Legal
Responsibility

Introduction

Leroy Powell was thoroughly drunk when he stumbled out into the
street. He was arrested for being disorderly in public, tried, and convicted. It seemed hardly a novel or interesting affair. But the case
reached the U.S. Supreme Court and resulted in a sharply divided
court and a landmark decision.[1]

Powell's defense at the trial was a novel one. His lawyers argued
that he was an alcoholic and that such bouts of drunkenness were the
norm for him. They further argued that alcoholism is a disease whose
major symptom is the inability to refrain from heavy drinking. Thus
his being in the street was the involuntary symptom of a mental disease. In short, Powell's defense was that he could not be held criminally responsible for behavior that was a symptom of a disease.

In the context of the 1960s it was becoming increasingly accepted
that alcoholism is indeed a disease and therefore deserves medical
attention. This was a firm rejection of the previously widely held view
that alcoholism is a condition due to moral depravity. It seemed that
the *Powell* case was an opportunity for the Supreme Court to abandon an outdated moralistic approach and recognize alcoholism as a
medical problem, not a criminal one.

This is a substantially revised version of "The Perils of Powell," *Harvard Law Review*
83 (1970): 793–812.

The Court voted four in favor of Powell's defense, four against, and one separate and ambivalent opinion.[2] The mere vote tally, however, does not show how precarious was the Court's refusal to adopt the precedents from the earlier cases. Four justices rejected the defense, viewing the disease concept of alcoholism as lacking a scientific basis. Four justices accepted the disease concept of alcoholism as true and as implying the involuntariness of the conduct. In their vigorous opinion written by Justice Fortas, they therefore urged reversal of Powell's conviction. In a separate opinion, Justice White appeared to accept and surely expressed sympathy for the disease and involuntariness theory of the defense. However, he felt that the facts developed at trial did not clearly correspond to the facts that the disease theory requires. Therefore he could not vote to overturn the conviction. As a consequence, the appeal was rejected and the conviction sustained. In spite of this division of opinion, the *Powell* case established the precedent rejecting the disease concept of alcoholism as a defense to criminal charges.

In *Driver v. Hinnant*[3] and *Easter v. District of Columbia*,[4] landmark cases decided not long before *Powell*, the courts had accepted the disease concept. Thus it was contrary to the utterly confident expectations of a number of specialists in this area of law that the Supreme Court rejected Powell's appeal, five to four.

Two decades later, a "disease concept of alcoholism" argument was offered in a civil trial.[5] Two war veterans who were initially entitled to support from the Veterans Administration for their education delayed applying. When the ten-year door of opportunity had closed, they then belatedly applied. They argued that because of their disease—alcoholism—they had been unable to apply in time. They therefore requested exemption from the time limitation.

The Veterans Administration rejected their appeal, holding to its general rule that alcoholism is not a disease. This VA rule was upheld on appeal to the District of Columbia Appellate Court. The case went to the Supreme Court, which also rejected the appeal on the ground that there is not a scientific consensus on these issues, and therefore the VA ruling was reasonable. So the disease concept of alcoholism lost out in both criminal and civil law.

Yet it still remains a widely accepted doctrine among the lay public and in wide medical circles. The divergence of opinions is sharp. Are the courts behind the times? Or have they examined the evidence well and judged correctly? Are those who accept the disease concept confused about the evidence, or are they enlightened?

It is my aim here to point out inadequacies in the structure of the *Powell* opinions accepting the disease concept of alcoholism. I will document in some detail that "involuntariness" and "disease" are dangerously slippery concepts and are not appropriate in this context.

Alcoholism as "Involuntary"

One factual premise of the argument of *Driver*, *Easter*, and the *Powell* dissent is that alcoholism is a "disease" that is "involuntarily" and nonculpably caused and maintained.[6]

This premise, which the courts seem to consider a unitary "concept,"[7] can of course be analyzed—at least superficially and maybe also more fundamentally—into two approaches. One rests on the key word "disease" and the other on "involuntary."

The *Powell* dissent deals with the problem of public drunkenness in terms of the second concept mentioned above, "involuntariness." The legal conclusion that resultant public intoxication cannot be made criminal then follows from the principle adopted by the *Powell* dissent that "[c]riminal penalties may not be inflicted upon a person for being in a condition he is powerless to change."[7]

I wish in the remainder of this chapter to examine the conceptual and factual foundation for the claims that alcoholism is a "disease" and that alcoholism, and the alcoholic's excessive drinking, are "involuntary." Specifically, I will first comment briefly on the *Powell* dissent's conception of those statements, and the factual support they offer, and then explore at greater length the relevant medical literature.

The "Hard Facts" of "Chronic Alcoholism"

The dissent accepts, without evaluative comment,[8] the trial judge's "findings of fact"[9]:

1. That chronic alcoholism is a disease which destroys the afflicted person's will power to resist the constant, excessive consumption of alcohol.

2. That a chronic alcoholic does not appear in public by his own volition
    but under a compulsion symptomatic of the disease of chronic alco-
    holism.
3. That Leroy Powell . . . is a chronic alcoholic who is afflicted with the
    disease of chronic alcoholism.

Four of the Justices who reject Powell's appeal agree that these are
not "findings of fact" in "any recognizable, traditional sense in which
that term has been used in a court of law."[10] The first two of the
"findings" constitute sweepingly general assertions about a large class
of alcoholics.[11] They assert that chronic alcoholism is itself an involuntarily maintained status and, further, that medical science has
demonstrated constant and inevitable relationships between this status and public drunkenness.

It is evident that no reasonable basis for such "findings" could
appear either in the testimony of Powell himself or the testimony
concerning his personal history. Conceivably the testimony of
expert witnesses might justify the findings—yet in Powell's trial
only one psychiatric expert testified. While this expert did in fact
testify to the effect that a "chronic alcoholic" is an "involuntary
drinker," his elaboration of this characterization obscured his
meaning.[12] In any event, inconclusive testimony by a single expert
witness could hardly justify even the findings as to involuntariness
(the expert said nothing of alcoholism as a "disease"). Such testimony would be persuasive only if there were a background of theory so familiar, unambiguous, and unchallengeable as to render further elaboration otiose. A major portion of the dissent consists of
an attempt to provide just such an appropriate medical background
as the "context" that the dissenters claim an understanding of the
case "requires."[13]

With respect to the medical background concerning "chronic
alcoholism," the *Powell* dissent acknowledges that "there is a great
deal that remains to be discovered," that "many aspects of the disease remain obscure," and that we are "woefully deficient in our
medical, diagnostic, and therapeutic knowledge" in both this area
and that of "mental disease."[14] Although this admission alone takes
much of the ground from beneath the sweeping "findings of fact"
of the trial judge, the dissent maintains that there are "some hard
facts—medical and, especially, legal facts—that are accessible to us

and that provide a context in which the instant case may be analyzed."[15]

One such "hard fact" appears to be that alcoholism is medically recognized as a disease.[16] The dissent also believes it to be a fact that the "core meaning" of the disease concept of alcoholism

> as agreed by authorities, is that alcoholism is caused and maintained by something other than the moral fault of the alcoholic, something that, to a greater or lesser extent depending upon the physiological or psychological makeup and history of the individual, cannot be controlled by him.[17]

Neither of these "facts" mentions public intoxication. This is not because the "core meaning" merely happens to be formulated in the dissent as a very general statement, but because, as we shall see in detail later, its statement can only be a very general one.[18]

Though the "core meaning" is silent with respect to the symptoms or effects of alcoholism, or their voluntariness, it does raise the issue of voluntariness with respect to the causes of the status of chronic alcoholism and with respect to the persistence of that status. However, what it says is not that an alcoholic's condition is involuntary, but that an alcoholic's control over what causes his "disease" will be a matter of "greater or lesser degree." The degree cannot be assessed in general for all "chronic alcoholics" but will depend upon the individual alcoholic's physiology, psychological makeup, and personal history. Such cautiousness contrasts sharply with the blunt conclusions of the trial judge and of the dissenters themselves that alcoholism is "involuntary."

Even more injudiciously blunt is the judgment that however alcoholism be caused, it is in any event not attributable to "the moral fault of the alcoholic."[20] The pontifical tone may be due in part to the fact that while medical doctors do have a certain expertise in studying causation, it is not, as medical scientists are themselves prone to insist, moral expertise. Expertise generates a sensitivity to the complexity of issues and a consequent cautiousness when generalizing on those issues; beyond the area of our expertise we tend to be freer with wholesale judgments. In fact, of course, moral exculpation is hardly a proper part of medical theory, and to offer it as medically established "fact" is on its face unjustifiable.

The "Voluntariness" Approach

Such inconsistencies and logical difficulties indicate that there may be underlying, unacknowledged factors influencing the dissent's conclusions. We shall discuss some of these factors in the next section, when we examine the significance of the widespread medical acceptance of the proposition that alcoholism is a disease. For the present, we shall focus on the "voluntariness" approach by looking to the medical literature.

Many of the leading health authorities view "loss of control" as the "hallmark" of alcoholism.[19] The assertion is sufficiently widespread to give the impression of substantial agreement among many authorities, and it has nearly self-evident moral and legal implications to persons of goodwill. The *Powell* dissent is not unique in culminating its discussion of "loss of control" by quoting from a medical source: "the main point for the non-professional is that alcoholism is not within the control of the person involved."[20]

However, concepts that center around voluntariness, as do all questions of psychological fact, present some of the most complex issues in both law and ethics. A phrase like "I couldn't control myself" or "I had no choice" could express variously a physical incapacity, unconsciousness, incapacity to conform due to mental illness, somnambulism,[21] involuntary intoxication,[22] extreme provocation, or the necessity to act to save life or to act with little time to reflect. Some of these circumstances could serve in some jurisdictions as a complete defense to criminal liability. In others it could be a complete defense in certain factual contexts. Or it could serve as a "partial" defense, in some degree mitigating culpability. In still other contexts it would have no legal effect but might mitigate punishment. These very different senses of self-control by no means exhaust the range of meanings.

In what sense, then, do the authorities on alcoholism speak of "loss of control" in connection with chronic alcoholism? The *Powell* dissent's categorical claim that alcoholism is not within the alcoholic's control dissolves into multiple ambiguities, given the very different things that authorities mean by the phrase. Moreover, there are different sorts of facts that purportedly justify it, and a variety of substantive qualifications ultimately appended. Finally, the *Powell* dissent ignores the authoritative literature in which the phrase is conspicuously omitted or explicitly rejected.

From still another standpoint it is difficult to sustain any categorical statements about alcoholism in light of the multiplicity of diagnostic schemes. Plaut says that "the term 'alcoholism' should be used with awareness that this condition is not always easy to diagnose or to be distinguished from other types of problem drinking. In addition, even those to whom the diagnosis is correctly given still differ greatly from one another and are likely to require different types of treatment and assistance."[23]

Jellinek distinguishes and lists over one hundred hypotheses about the nature of alcoholism.[24] There is not even any substantial agreement about the field of knowledge from which the best understanding of alcoholism may be forthcoming. Hypotheses range from the genetic through the physiological and pharmacological to the psychological and sociological.

It is still more damaging to the "involuntariness" argument that no expert would dispute that variations in the patterns of drinking among alcoholics are myriad. Most would agree that what alcoholics have in common is simply "a heavy preoccupation with drinking."[25] In some cultural groups this often leads to serious disturbances in social adaptation.[26]

Thus it is not surprising that many authorities who use "loss of control" language ultimately introduce serious qualifications. One of the leading authorities who holds "loss of control" to be the "pathagnomonic symptom" of alcoholism does not mean by this phrase that the person cannot abstain or cannot stop once he has started drinking. Rather, we are told, the phrase means that "it is not certain that [the alcoholic] will be able to stop at will."[27] Indeed, in France and other beer and wine drinking countries a predominant pattern of alcoholism is the constant, daily drinking of wine, with "inability to abstain," but with control over the amount drunk at any one time so that drunkenness or incapacity to carry on with the day's activities is rare. Cessation of drinking does produce withdrawal symptoms, however.[28]

Another authority who uses "loss of control" as a "criterion" for diagnosing alcoholism tells us that in various "protected" situations (among them incidentally, the prison) many alcoholics will with "little or no difficulty" abstain or stop.[29] Still other authorities characterize "loss of control" as "not an all-or-none phenomenon"[30] and "a relative and variable phenomenon."

In short, we are told not that the alcoholic has *no* control of his drinking, but that he has greater or lesser control, *widely* varying in degree according to the circumstances and the individual. This consensus conforms with the "core meaning" of the "disease concept of alcoholism" summarized in the *Powell* dissent. For the dissent states that the alcoholic's inability to control his drinking can exist to a "greater or lesser extent depending on the physiological or psychological makeup and history of the individual." This, however, is inconsistent with the *Powell* dissent, and the *Driver* and *Easter* opinions, insofar as they assume that all chronic alcoholics are, by virtue of their being such, without power to control their drinking.

The frequent reference to alcoholism as an "addiction"[31] may seem to settle the volitional issue. Yet the World Health Organization's Expert Committee on Dependence-Producing Drugs recently abandoned the term "addiction,"[32] proposing instead a series of terms connoting different kinds and degrees of drug "dependence." The proposed terms range from mere "desire" through a "strong desire or need" to "overpowering desire or need."[33]

It follows that we must ask in what way and in what degree an alcoholic is thought to be alcohol-dependent. Among those who incline to some form of "loss of control" characterization, a number maintain the cause is a "physical" or "physiological mechanism."[34] As to the nature of this mechanism, there is a wide variety of opinion. The range of hypotheses include theories about genetic, neurological, metabolic, or allergic abnormalities which create a peculiar vulnerability to alcohol. And while the word "physical" would appear to exclude meaningful choice, the specific hypotheses, as we have seen, are never that simple. Far from excluding volition, most consist of complex models that more or less explicitly include volition along with the physical causes.

In fact, there is universal agreement that alcohol is not as physiologically dependence-producing as the morphine narcotics. Although it is often said that after one drink, the alcoholic feels a physical demand for the drug so strong that she cannot stop short of intoxication, Merry has provided persuasive experimental evidence to the contrary.[35] Beyond this threshold agreement, some theories postulate a physically induced craving for alcohol. Others speak of craving for the state of intoxication rather than for the liquor. Some theories hypothesize a physically induced craving to begin drinking, whereas others assume control over the taking of a first drink, but with some loss of control over further drinking. Moreover, some theorists view compulsion to keep drinking as due to a destruction of certain control centers in the brain, or as an involuntary, conditioned response to incipient withdrawal symptoms. Others view this compulsion as only a learned, somewhat controllable preference for continued drinking. Finally, many of the "physical" hypotheses suppose that continued drinking produces a gradual physical change in the alcoholic. Therefore the compulsion to drink increases over time.

Obviously, the moral and legal implications of these various hypotheses may be quite different. If, for example, a physical craving for alcohol triggers a specific, automatic reflex of drinking alcohol, then we exclude by hypothesis any significant volition. To the extent such a reflex cannot be demonstrated, then we deal with volitional response to a desire.

With respect to the many hypotheses that postulate no initial physical craving, but only a physical process that compels continued drinking once started, the following question arises. Do the alcoholics themselves believe they can stop, and to what extent is that belief reasonable? The expert in *Powell* testified that many alcoholics do believe they can stop drinking, but that belief is not always true. Finally, some hypotheses find volition throughout the drinking pattern, conceiving both the initiation and continuance of drinking as volitional responses to a more or less compelling desire.

Hypotheses that stress involuntariness must contend with the fact that many alcoholics do choose to abstain or control their drinking. This may be only occasionally, as is often true with chronic alcoholics.[36] Or it may be in some more permanent way, such as a personal decision to abstain, or seeking medical or psychological help, or by joining such groups as Alcoholics Anonymous or Synanon. Of course, capacity to resist the urge to drink on one occasion or for a period of time does not imply that the alcoholic will have such capacity at other times. However, an alcoholic who enjoyed periods of abstinence, or who could be supposed capable of voluntarily subjecting herself to a "cure," would not readily be found nonresponsible.

It remains a central feature of most of the "physical" hypotheses that the alcoholic, though in some way peculiarly sensitive physically to alcohol, is one who faces a very difficult and painful choice. I am not arguing that any of these hypotheses is false, though it is important to keep in mind that they often conflict with each other and that none has been confirmed.[37] My purpose here is to indicate that "physical" hypotheses do not claim that the alcoholic has no volitional control over drinking. Their claim is that, partly because of physical abnormality, the alcoholic is one who faces a choice that is (increasingly) more difficult than for most people.

Moreover, many of the contemporary hypotheses that are influential in the health professions, though they may speak of "loss of control" (quite a number do not), ascribe this to psychological or social conditions rather than physical ones. Here a term such as "compulsive" may again be used, though some authorities say improperly so.[38] But we must look behind the metaphor.

Pattison refers to alcoholism as a "psychosocial behavior syndrome" and asserts that the taking of alcohol is primarily a "central integrative symbol around which the person organizes his life."[39] Or, as another physician puts it: "[A]lcoholism is . . . only a 'common path' in the way of problem solving to a number of adaptational issues. . . ."[40]

We should not be misled by the technical psychological and sociological language. This latter group of authorities is simply saying that, on the whole, the alcoholic has chosen this way to handle his problems in life. It is supposed that the more he does so, the more he has a stake in this approach and a deep fear and dislike for any other. To say "he can't control it" amounts in this context to saying that mere moralistic appeals of the usual kind by family and friends are not likely to succeed. Nor are subvocal or vocal "resolutions" by the person himself likely to be effective. Excessive drinking has become his "way of life" in spite of such appeals and resolutions. But it remains possible that other kinds of appeal, or a change in life setting, may successfully lead him to self-control. A way of life is not easily or casually changed. On the other hand, it is not something beyond volition.

The most persuasive testimony in support of this view comes, unwittingly at times, from the advocates of the various "loss of control" hypotheses. When we look to the therapeutic techniques that these advocates propose or acknowledge as most effective, we see that they involve appeals for the alcoholic to adopt voluntarily one or another program of reform. These advocates appeal to him to enter voluntarily a "protective setting" such as a hospital and to abide voluntarily by its rules against drinking. Or they appeal to him to enter voluntarily and cooperatively on a course of Antabuse, "reconditioning," or membership in Alcoholics Anonymous.[41] Most of these programs, in spite of their "loss of control" doctrines, require the alcoholic to voluntarily cease drinking as a condition of entering and remaining in the program. There are, however, leading authorities who explicitly recommend coercive pressures to get the alcoholic to control his drinking.[42]

The effectiveness of noncoercive abstinence rules shows that drinking is to some significant degree volitional, the key being the social context and motives rather than a generalized inability to stop drinking.

I have translated the technical language, including the necessary qualifications, to formulate a statement in harmony with a large number of influential hypotheses about alcoholism:

> *Possibly partly due to some abnormal physical condition, chronic alcoholics are those who for any of a variety of other reasons have increasingly preferred drinking as a way of adapting to their life-problems. They have reached the point where the personal and social consequences of their drinking require them to make a choice. The choice to stop drinking, though usually practicable, is distressing and difficult, both physically and mentally. It may be very helpful to have the aid of special encouragement, an appropriate environment, professional guidance, or moderate coercive influences.*

Alcoholism as a "Disease"

The second "medical fact" is the simple formula "alcoholism is a disease." This probably has done most to foster the intuitive notion that alcoholism is not an appropriate object for criminal punishment. The dissenting opinion notes at the very outset of its statement of "hard facts" about alcoholism that "[i]n 1956 the [AMA] for the first time designated alcoholism as a major medical problem. . . . This significant development marked the acceptance among the medical profession of the 'disease concept of alcoholism.'"[43]

I intend to show that the widespread (but by no means universal) acceptance in the medical and health professions of the "disease concept of alcoholism" reflects a variety of considerations. Some are legitimate and important to the *health* professions. However, none of these considerations has any obvious bearing on the legal issue of punishability under the Eighth Amendment. Nor do they have any bearing on the scientific understanding of chronic heavy drinking.

One such consideration is the underlying judgment, with which I concur, that it is reasonable for the health professions to try to help with the problem of alcoholism. Certainly the symptoms of heavy intoxication or withdrawal from alcohol may need immediate medical attention. Another important consideration is the widespread hope and expectation that the medical profession will someday develop more effective remedies for alcohol abuse. While there is no doubt about the importance and inspirational efficacy of this expectation,[44] these hopes are not obviously relevant to the propriety of punishing alcoholics.

There are certain ancillary practical considerations that also motivate acceptance among doctors of "the disease concept." In the first place, it is evidently in the interest of the medical attack on alcoholism that large sums of money be reliably accessible to researchers and therapists. Adherence within the profession to such formulas as "alcoholism is a disease" (or an "illness," or a "medical problem") does much to provide assurance to such fund-granting agencies. Such assurance was no doubt profoundly strengthened, as intended, when the medical profession in 1956 formally and clearly expressed its concern to assume a responsibility for dealing with alcoholism.[45] Similarly, the availability of hospitals for the medical effort against alcoholism was apparently facilitated by the official declaration of the AMA.[46] It also helps the effort to motivate more medical doctors to assume responsibility for treating alcoholics. Acknowledgment of the reluctance of both psychiatric and nonpsychiatric clinicians to accept chronic alcoholics as patients is a commonplace in the literature.[47]

It is also extremely important to doctors dealing with alcoholics that the general public support their efforts. The official AMA announcement and the wide professional use in public discussion of the formula "alcoholism is a disease" have been vital to the growing public support of medical research in the area.[48] The medical profession's public use of the phrase has been a powerful influence in combating a major cultural obstacle to their efforts—the public's habitual allegiance to "moralistic" approaches. Many health authorities feel that moral, religious, and penal approaches have failed. They see public commitment to these approaches as a major diversion of effort, money, and resources from the medical effort. There is also a profound but usually tacit moral judgment on the part of many health professionals that the condemnatory and penal approach is inhumane. Once again, however, these considerations, justified or not, have no bearing on the scientific understanding of alcoholism.

Nor should one ignore the professional and financial stakes in what has become a rehabilitation industry employing many thousands of professionals and semiprofessionals, and generating many hundreds of millions of dollars in income. This industry depends on acceptance of the "disease concept of alcoholism."

This is not the place to discuss the concept of "disease" in general.[49] However, I do wish to direct attention to the well-known attempt by Jellinek to clarify the factual content of the disease concept of alcoholism.[50] His attempt concludes almost as quickly as it begins. After noting the circularity and unhelpful generality of the medical dictionary definitions of disease, Jellinek concludes: "*[A] disease is what the medical profession recognizes as such*. . . . [T]hrough this fact alone alcoholism becomes an illness, whether a part of the lay public likes it or not, and even if a minority of the medical profession is disinclined to accept the idea."[51]

In general, I do not believe that anything I have said precludes the many legislative options for establishing rational procedures and institutions, penal or civil, for dealing with the alcoholic. Nor is there any support in anything I have said for the all too common irrational, expensive, and inhumane harassment of the alcoholic. Such treatment, especially of the impoverished and alienated alcoholic, is still prevalent.[52]

The burden of my remarks is, however, that the prevailing climate of opinion about alcoholism is a gravely defective basis for public policy. The "disease concept of alcoholism" is essentially a public relations formula without scientific foundation. The slogans about the alcoholic's inability to exert any effective control over drinking are demonstrably false. Medical care for the physical and mental suffering of the habitual heavy drinker is surely desirable. But dealing with the habit itself is not rational if conducted on the basis of the disease concept and related notions.

The Concept of
Mental Disorder

Introduction

John S. is an English rare book collector. He has a room lined with
original or signed editions from the Guttenberg era to the present day.
We are awed and impressed. In China, Wang is a book-burner. He has
just ceremonially burned his moisture-degraded set of Hsun-Tzu's
works. This is the traditional Chinese way to abandon unusable
books, since books are revered and cannot simply be thrown away. We
respect Wang. Aki is a Kwakiutl Indian who burns up much of his
family wealth in the presence of his tribe members. This traditional
gesture brings him great respect and status within the tribe.

Eli W. is another story. He is an American who keeps all the news-
papers, magazines, and other publications he receives. Eventually his
apartment is so jammed full that there is no room for him. He is
forced to sleep in the cold damp basement, where he soon develops
pneumonia. Eli W. is, obviously, crazy. Or if one prefers more genteel
language, he is mentally ill.

What is the significant difference between John S., Wang, and Aki,
on one hand, and Eli W. on the other? How can we negotiate the line
between psychopathology and behavior stemming from rational
choice? Eli's case is discussed in the *DSM-IV Casebook*.[1] The *Casebook*
in turn is the companion to the official *Diagnostic and Statistical
Manual of Mental Disorders* (1994) of the American Psychiatric
Association (DSM-IV).

The *Casebook*'s expert diagnosticians considered some plausible diagnoses for Eli W., diagnoses such as Obsessive-Compulsive Personality Disorder. On careful consideration, however, they could not find a specific diagnosis that would adequately fit Eli W.'s case. They opted finally for the more or less empty label, "Anxiety Disorder Not Otherwise Specified or Personality Disorder Not Otherwise Specified."

Plainly, even in the absence of a meaningful diagnosis, they appreciated that Eli W. was mentally disordered. How did the diagnosticians know? What was it specifically about his conduct that signaled to them that this conduct manifested mental disorder? It was intuitively clearly evident to them. Indeed, it would be intuitively evident to almost anyone. But what is the basis of that intuition? In a nutshell, what is meant by "mental disorder"?

Perhaps, one surmises, there's something amiss in the way Eli W.'s brain is working. This may indeed be the case, and if so it may be the cause of his irrational behavior. Yet this doesn't answer our question. For we recognize that he's crazy by observing his conduct, yet we know nothing about his brain processes or any other possible causes.

Whatever the causes may be—and we commonly don't know—the presence of mental disorder must lie in something that has to do with our observation of Eli W.'s conduct. It is only when we have identified his conduct as irrational that we then become interested in the causes of such behavior.

True enough, we have not specified precisely what it is about such conduct that marks Eli W. as mentally disordered. Perhaps we should turn to the experts for a precise statement of what it is about conduct that marks it as a manifestation of mental disorder.

"Mental Disorder": The Elusive Definition

The American Psychiatric Association's DSM-IV[2] provides the authoritative diagnostic schema for U.S. psychiatrists.[*] In its intro-

---

[*]DSM-IV-TR, published six years after the original DSM-IV, consists of textual revisions that make no substantive change in conceptual or textual matters of concern here. The same is true of the two editions of the *Casebook* that correspond to these two editions of DSM-IV.

ductory remarks on the meaning of "mental disorder," the DSM-IV says, "no definition adequately specifies precise boundaries for the concept of 'mental disorder.'"[3] Indeed, this admission is followed by a warning: "individuals sharing a diagnosis are likely to be heterogeneous even in regard to the defining features of the diagnosis. . . ."[4]

Undaunted, the editors speak of this lack of any coherent definition as providing "flexibility."[5] So it is not surprising that the number of pages in the psychiatric diagnostic manual grew from 295 pages in 1952[6] to 636 pages in the 1994 version of DSM-IV. Nor can it be viewed with equanimity that recently over 50 million Americans are reported by the Surgeon General to be mentally disordered.[7]

How do the editors of DSM-IV decide what conditions to include among the mental disorders? They consider a certain amount of behavioral data. Yet they also acknowledge using "historical" considerations, which is to say they give weight to psychiatric tradition. In addition, they say they use "common sense."[8] Though they do not say so, the fact is that on occasion political, factional, and moral disputes play a role in the decision-making.[9] In short, there is a lot of what they characterize as "flexibility."

The editors of DSM-IV remark that, in any case, their definition is as useful as any other available definition and has helped to guide decisions regarding which conditions on the boundary between normality and pathology should be included in DSM-IV.[10] This latter remark assures us that while the DSM-IV lacks an adequate definition, no better definition is available.

The present study is intended to fill the gap and provide an adequate definition. The definition to be proposed here shows clearly the difference between behavior manifesting mental disorder and behavior that does not. It amounts to a vindication of the concept actually used in DSM-IV, though it is used there intuitively and not always used reliably by diagnosticians. The definition that I will propose here reflects common usage as well. Moreover, it clearly supports the view that mental disorders are indeed objectively existing conditions, not "myths" as claimed by the so-called antipsychiatry movement.[11] And it avoids the pseudoscience of definitions purportedly based on the theory of evolution.[12]

DSM-IV: The Blind Alleys

ATTEMPTS AT A GENERAL DEFINITION

Although the editors often speak of "the definition," it becomes evident that they have suggested a plurality of definitions, and that "each of the definitions offered is a useful indicator for a mental disorder, but none is equivalent to the concept, and different situations call for different definitions."[13]

Indeed, as we have been told, individuals with the same diagnosis may in fact be heterogeneous in regard to the defining features of the diagnosis. Thus when we look for a general definition of "mental disorder," we are told that DSM-IV employs an inadequate and unspecified heterogeneity of definitions. The editors comment favorably in this connection as a situation that allows "flexibility."[14] Failing to find a general definition, we can examine a number of the more particular comments made in the course of the DSM-IV discussions.

FROM THE GENERAL TO THE SPECIFIC

> In DSM-IV, each of the mental disorders is conceptualized as a *clinically significant* behavioral or psychological syndrome or pattern that occurs in an individual. . . .[15]

This clinical significance criterion "helps establish the threshold for the diagnosis of a disorder."[16] By use of it we can distinguish mental disorder from a "symptomatic presentation" that "is not *inherently pathological*" and thus does not warrant a diagnosis of disorder.[17]

How are we to identify this crucial property of being "clinically significant"? DSM-IV gives no definition of this phrase in its glossary of technical terms. And what does it mean to say that symptoms may not be "inherently pathological"? The term "pathological" is neither defined nor explained, much less the import of "inherently."

Both "clinically significant" and "pathological" seem on their face to be question-begging. We have no definitions or explanations of their meaning. Of course if we could identify certain conduct as evidence of mental disorder, we could then say it is clinically significant or pathological. But we do not know whether certain conduct is evidence of mental disorder unless we know that it is pathological or clinically significant. In short, we are going in circles. Not surprisingly, the editors acknowledge that the identification of clinical significance in a particular case can call for an "inherently difficult clinical judgment."[18]

While DSM-IV does not succeed in providing a general definition, it does contain what is presumably intended as a helpful general comment. The editors explain that a clinically significant behavior pattern is "*associated* with present distress (e.g., a painful symptom) or disability (i.e., impairment in one or more important areas of functioning) or with a significantly increased risk of suffering, death, pain, disability, or an important loss of freedom."[19]

"Associated" in what way? The term is all-encompassing. We are given no guidance as to the nature of the association. Does it refer to identity, causality, constant conjunction, significant correlation, necessary condition, past, present, or future? True, one might infer that a pattern is not clinically significant if none of DSM-IV's mentioned conditions obtains. But on the other hand, we could equally well find that such conditions do obtain, yet not be properly associated with clinically significant behavior.

The fact is that the symptoms said to be associated with clinical significance are also frequently associated with patterns that obviously are not clinically significant. "Present distress," for example, need not be associated with clinically significant or pathological behavior. It may just as well be an accompaniment to the grief and frustration common in human life. "Present distress" is also associated with the physical pains incidental to accidental injury or physical ailment of everyday life.

DSM-IV also states that clinical significance is associated with certain major risks. But the risks mentioned are equally present in such common but not necessarily pathological behaviors as dangerous sports, dishonest activities, disputes, failed relationships, harming loved ones, and negligence in handling machinery.

In the attempt to clarify matters, the editors note that "whatever its original cause, [the pattern of behavior] must currently be considered a manifestation of a behavioral, psychological, or biological dysfunction in the individual. . . ."[20] The phrase "behavioral, psychological, or biological" covers everything and therefore merely tells us that there is something or other wrong with the individual. The potentially useful message in this remark thus turns on the word "dysfunction."

Once again we need to ask: How shall we know if some behavioral, psychological, or biological pattern is dysfunctional? The term is not defined in the glossary, though it is crucial throughout the DSM-IV discussions of mental disorder.

DSM-IV seems to give an indirect clue to the meaning of "dysfunction" when it says that "neither deviant behavior (e.g., political, religious, or sexual) nor conflicts that are primarily between the individual and society are mental disorders unless the deviance or conflict is a symptom of *dysfunction in the individual, as described above.*"[21]

When we examine what is "described above," we find it to be the statement that mental disorder must be "a behavioral, psychological, or biological dysfunction in the individual."[22] We are going around in verbal circles.

In summary, the concept of mental disorder is not defined or adequately explained in DSM-IV.

DSM-IV: Clues to the Answer

Although DSM-IV fails to provide a satisfactory definition of "mental disorder," it does tacitly employ a valid concept.

One important and helpful comment in DSM-IV is as follows: "In addition, this syndrome or pattern must not be merely an expectable and culturally sanctioned response to a particular event, for example, the death of a loved one . . . it must currently be considered a manifestation of . . . dysfunction in the individual."[23]

While we do not yet know what "dysfunction in the individual" means, we now know, specifically, that "expectable" and "culturally sanctioned" behavior is not dysfunctional. What do these terms signify?

Obviously "expectable" does not mean "expected." Even behavior that is not expected is usually normal. "Expectable," as the suffix implies, means that the behavior *could* be expected. That is, even if it is not expected, it is a practice recognized within the person's culture.

The latter comment, in turn, expresses the meaning of "culturally sanctioned." There are several possible dictionary meanings of "sanctioned." Clearly it can mean but in this context does not mean "punished" or "forbidden." Although "sanctioned" can also mean "approved," it cannot take this meaning here. Behavior that is not approved is not necessarily a sign of mental disorder.

"Sanctioned" makes sense here, however, if what the editors mean is something like "recognized"—that is, not only identified but also granted a certain authoritative status. It is a recognized practice in the cultural repertoire. Here, as the dictionary says, "recognized" has a special force. Thus we say, George W. Bush was declared victor over Al Gore and recognized as President. Conduct that we recognize or sanction is conduct that we acknowledge to have the status of being a practice of our culture. It is distinguished from conduct that is not recognized as one of the cultural practices, and in that respect has no meaningful place within the culture.

For example, Jones makes a moderately offensive remark to Smith, who thereupon throws a punch at Jones. This may not be conduct that is approved, but it is certainly something that could be expected. It is an act that is recognizable as a practice, however deplorable, of our culture.

Suppose, however, that Jones makes the same mildly insulting remark to Smith, and Smith reacts by shouting that Jones must be an agent of the Devil sent to haunt him. Whereupon Smith takes out a gun and shoots Jones. In the cultural context, this is not something expectable. (But shooting someone for even a mild insult might be expectable in a youth gang subculture.)

The preceding explanations suffer from the difficulty that we have no term in English that quite fits the concept at issue. Both "expectable" and "culturally sanctioned" can mislead. Such terms as "meaningful," "intelligible," or "comprehensible" have also been used in their place.[24] But each of these terms can mislead. For each could also apply to Smith's paranoid conduct, since we do understand that he is fearful, angry, and is purposely shooting Jones.

"Irrational" is another term that has been proposed to connote the distinctive characteristic of conduct resulting from mental disorder.[25] But here, too, there is ambiguity. Foolish conduct can be called irrational without meaning that it manifests mental disorder. We might call a person irrational for having borrowed money excessively, but we need not mean to imply mental disorder.

One of the tasks of the present inquiry is to find a way of aptly characterizing what DSM-IV calls dysfunction, pathology, or mental disorder. This is not a matter of mere words. It calls for specifying the objective characteristics that we intuitively recognize as the signs of mental disorder. We must return to DSM-IV for further clues to those objective characteristics.

The general introductory remarks in DSM-IV include the following:

> A clinician who is unfamiliar with nuances of an individual's cultural frame of reference may incorrectly judge as psychopathology those normal variations in behavior, belief, or experience that are particular to the individual's culture. For example, certain religious practices or beliefs (e.g., seeing or hearing a deceased relative during bereavement) may be misdiagnosed as manifestations of a psychotic disorder.[26]

This proposition has a corollary. If the behavior, beliefs, and experiences of an individual are expectable and sanctioned *in that individual's particular culture*, then these are not evidence of mental disorder. Yet, as usual, DSM-IV implicitly limits the cultural reference to *other* cultures. The U.S. culture is tacitly taken as the norm. DSM-IV fails to recognize that U.S. culture is thereby given an unwarranted privileged status. If the diagnosis of mental disorder can depend on the "particulars of the individual's culture," should not U.S. culture be included?

DSM-IV is the first edition of the DSM series that gives culture a significant place in diagnosis. It takes account of culture in two ways. There is an appendix listing "Culture-Bound Syndromes," that is, indigenous patterns peculiar to various cultures foreign to the United States. There is also a new special subsection in each diagnostic category, "Specific Culture, Age, and Gender Features." This subcategory concerns "variations in the presentation of the disorder that may be attributable to the individual's cultural setting. . . ."[27]

Thus, in spite of the increased recognition, DSM-IV still treats culture as ancillary. The standard syndromes that occupy the main body of the text are presumably not "culture-bound" because they belong to U.S. culture. Yet it should be clear that in order to recognize that a patient is not from a foreign culture or a U.S. subculture, one must have recognized that the patient is from the mainstream U.S. culture. If that is so, then the diagnostic question has to be whether the patient's conduct is expectable from the standpoint of U.S. culture.

To use the example in the preceding quotation, how would one know whether the delusion of a person who claims to be hearing a deceased relative is evidence of mental disorder? As DSM-IV says, in order to make that decision one has to know whether the person belongs to a culture other than mainstream U.S. culture, and if so, whether such hallucination is the norm for that person's culture. Thus cultural reference is necessary in the diagnosis of all individual symptoms. A few further examples can help confirm this conclusion.

For example, "excessive" is an adjective essential to identifying a number of particular symptoms. Separation Anxiety Disorder is defined as "recurrent excessive distress. . . ." The same disorder has as a symptom "persistent and excessive worry. . . ."[28]

"Excessive" and quasi-synonymous terms are used as key qualifiers in the Phobias, Anxiety Disorders, and Adjustment Disorders. Impulse Control Disorder is identifiable if the response is "grossly out of control." Symptomatic of Learning Disorders is performance that is "substantially below what is expected. . . ." "Often" and "frequent" are essential qualifiers in the Conduct Disorders. The Sexual Disorders are defined not only in terms of "clinical significance," but also as "persistent and recurring," while a defining term in the Personality Disorders is "pervasive."

All these qualifiers[29] are inherently culture dependent. For example, whether reading or speaking are "substantially below what is expected" can only be determined by reference to the individual's culture. Whether a sexual behavior pattern should be characterized as "persistent and recurring" in the pathological sense can vary from one culture to another. The public wailing and gesturing of a Middle Eastern woman who is grieving is not excessive in the context of her culture. However it would probably be pathologically "excessive" for an Anglo-American.

Unusually lengthy remarks about culture are made in the DSM-IV discussion of schizophrenia:

> Ideas that may appear to be delusional in one culture (e.g., sorcery and witchcraft) may be commonly held in another. In some cultures, visual or auditory hallucinations with a religious content may be a normal part of religious experience . . . in addition the assessment of disorganized speech may be made difficult by linguistic variation in narrative styles across cultures. . . . The assessment of affect requires sensitivity to differences in styles of emotional expression, eye contact, and body language which vary across cultures. . . . disturbances of volition must also be carefully assessed.[30]

In sum, as DSM-IV acknowledges, the general propositions about the meaning of mental disorder are inadequate. In addition, the more specific comments about key symptoms all make either tacit or explicit reference to the person's culture.

The Meaning of "Mental Disorder"

Because the words used to distinguish between the pathological and the nonpathological are all ambiguous and hence can be misleading, I propose to use the term "culture-alien."

"Alien" means "foreign." But the *Oxford English Dictionary* lists this meaning as only one of several, and not the first. It defines "alien" as meaning unfamiliar, unacceptable, or repugnant, "of another world." The Latin root of the word is "alius," meaning "other." Thus the term connotes the radical ideas of incompatibility and radical difference in kind. It is unlike the ambiguous generalities ("meaningless," "incomprehensible") that have been proposed as criteria of mental disorder. "Culture-alien," in contrast, points specifically to the clinically relevant feature of conduct: the break with culture. It makes explicit that the conduct has no place in the individual's "world," that is, in the repertoire of practices of the individual's culture. "Culture-alien" reveals clearly the sense in which dysfunctional conduct is not "expectable" or "culturally sanctioned."

This criterion remedies the failure of DSM-IV to recognize the complete generality of the reference to culture in all diagnosis. For it has been common (in the U.S.) that the patient and diagnostician share the same culture. In such cases the placing of the conduct in its cultural context will usually be intuitive. As a result the cultural reference is unnoticed. This, in turn, has typically blinded diagnosticians to the necessity of this reference.

The term "culture-alien" is not a definition of "mental disorder." It refers to the person's conduct. It provides the decisive distinguishing mark, that is, the criterion of mental disorder. If the person's conduct is culture-alien, then we infer that the person suffers from a mental disorder. Thus, the mental disorder itself is the mental condition that determines the culture-alien character of the conduct.

The distinctive role of this criterion is illustrated if, for example, we suppose that physicians have identified some abnormal condition of a particular person's brain. If the conduct that results from that brain condition is culture-alien, that causal condition constitutes the mental disorder. If, however, the abnormal brain condition does not cause culture-alien conduct, then it does not constitute a psychiatric disorder.

Thus, whether a mental disorder is essentially, or partly, or only minimally biological or psychological in nature, that nature is not what establishes its character as mental disorder. What identify the condition as a mental disorder are the objective, observable facts about the person's conduct in the context of the person's own culture. Indeed we do not need to know, and very often do not know, what the inner condition is. Nevertheless, if there is culture-alien conduct, we know there is mental disorder.

Is Culture-Alienation a "Relativistic" Concept?

It is easy to assume that if the criterion of mental disorder is culture-alien conduct, then the meaning of "mental disorder" depends upon the culture. This would be a fundamental error. The meaning of "mental disorder" as defined here remains the same whatever the person's culture. What can vary from culture to culture is whether a particular person's conduct is alien to that person's culture. That this relationship is the criterion of mental disorder remains unchanged whatever the culture.

As we have seen, certain hallucinations are normal in one culture but pathological in another. It is in this sense true that whether a certain person's hallucination is pathological or not is "relative" to culture.

Yet this language is vague and misleading. We do need to know the particular person's culture. However, the question is whether the hallucinating is culture-alien. That question remains unchanged no matter what the culture.

It may seem on its face that a syndrome such as schizophrenia is essentially culture-independent, that is, the same in any culture.[31] It is an archetype of a mental disorder. If we do define "schizophrenia" as a mental disorder, then it follows that hallucinating, a classic symptom of schizophrenia, is not necessarily always a symptom of schizophrenia. As even DSM-IV notes, "In some cultures, visual or auditory hallucinations with a religious content may be a normal part of religious experience" and hence not signs of mental disorder.

The important point is that having a single criterion of mental disorder, no matter what the culture, provides for diagnoses that are universally valid. Correct use of the culture-alien criterion will have the same result whatever the person's culture or that of the diagnostician.

The Rationale for Using the Criterion

Why is culture-alien conduct the criterion for determining whether there is something objectively wrong with the person's mind?

While the preceding analyses have shown that this criterion has been tacitly used all along, the question raised at this point is a different one: Why is this usage reasonable? The answer lies in the significance of culture for human nature.

Each human being grows up in a particular cultural setting and is profoundly shaped by it. Without such acculturation we lack an essential feature of human being. Through this acculturation one becomes civil-ized and achieves one's unique personal identity.

In spite of the enormous complexity of the cultural repertoires, most human beings master their own culture sufficiently well to act spontaneously. This is an achievement that we take for granted. However, some adults may have matured and attained adequate mastery, but from whatever causes have suffered a significant loss of that mastery. Or, as DSM-IV would put it, the behavior is dysfunctional. That is, it leads to culture-alien conduct.

Important as is the criterion of mental disorder—culture-alien conduct—it tells us only one thing. It tells us that there is something wrong with the person's mind. The criterion does not tell us the relevant mental or social causes of that conduct. Nor does it tell us what remedy might be effective. The occurrence of culture-alien conduct simply reveals that there is a disability in the way the individual's mind is functioning. Insofar as there is such alienation, there is incapacity to act as a responsible agent.

Yet, given culture-alien conduct, empirical inquiries into causes and remedies become relevant. These are tasks for biological and psychological professionals.

Another limitation that needs to be taken into account is that the concept of culture-alienation has not been exhaustively explained and analyzed here. More remains to be done in that regard. A few brief further comments are necessary, however.

"Culture" has been defined in a variety of ways, but in the present context it helps to see it as a repertoire of practices. For example, we greet people, we shake hands with people, we speak words of welcome, we clasp the hand we are shaking with greater or lesser firmness. These are recognizable and in this case interrelated practices in our culture.

Robbing a bank, though it is a morally and legally reprehensible practice, is nevertheless a recognized practice in the U.S. cultural repertoire. To ask whether certain behavior is culture-alien is not to ask whether it is objectionable. It may be; it may not be. That is not the issue. In any case, it is by definition not conduct that falls within the moral framework of the culture. Being culture-alien, it provides no basis for moral judgment one way or another.

Performing a practice is rarely a rigidly prescribed activity. Variation and innovation are normal. Mistakes and faulty performances also belong to a practice since we recognize them as such.

Conclusion

I believe that the concept developed here points the way to resolving many uncertainties. Uncertainties often surround the decision whether to consider a particular pattern of behavior as evidence of mental disorder. The culture-alien criterion resolves this difficulty. It can also minimize the confusion that too often arises when psychiatry and the law interact. In classifying mental disorders, it poses a factual question that can replace subjective and partisan decisions with science.

Does Coercion Negate Responsibility?

A desperate looking man steps swiftly out of the bank and startles the driver of a nearby parked car by hastily entering the car, pointing a gun at the driver's head, and ordering, "Get going—fast!" The driver tries to keep enough composure to put the car in motion and to speed away. Eventually the gun-wielder orders the driver to stop, abandons the car, and loses himself in a nearby department store crowd.

Eventually the district attorney's office must decide whether to prosecute the driver for assisting in a criminal act. Upon careful review of the facts, the attorney in charge of the case decides not to prosecute. Clearly the driver was coerced. Under such circumstances the verdict at trial, if the case were pursued, would inevitably be Not Guilty. The driver did commit a criminal act, but since the act was coerced, the driver is not criminally responsible.

We'll accept that judgment as fair. But why? What is it specifically about coercion that makes it fair and lawful to remove the burden of responsibility for an act? Is there a theory that explains this? Or is there nothing to say except, "It's intuition," "It's common sense"?

If we look to the law, there seems to be a theory widely shared by jurists as well as the lay public. The theory is that when threatened with dire injury or death as the instant alternative to obedience, a

This is a substantially revised version of "Victimization: A Legalist Analysis of Coercion, Deception, Undue Influence, and Excusable Prison Escape," *Washington and Lee Law Review* 42, no. 1 (1985): 65–118.

normal person's will is "overcome," it is "broken," "overpowered," "subverted," "pressured." A person in such a situation "has no choice" but to comply.[1]

Although expressed in idiomatic and differing language, the point of all such language seems reasonably clear and essentially the same in all versions. We are not concerned here with nuances but in the main idea proposed.

The universality of such language suggests that it is at least a plausible and probably correct explanation of the essence of coercion. In fact, however, the theory is false in its most central and fundamental meaning. It has no scientific or factual basis of any kind. More important yet, it is the wrong sort of explanation. At bottom it is an explanation in terms of individual psychology, the mental "forces" at work in and on the mind. Yet the true explanation, and the one that throws a certain light on the meaning of personal responsibility, is not a psychological one at all.

To understand coercion one must understand that what is at issue is not personal psychology but objective rationality. The aim in what follows is to show what this means, why it is true, and what it implies in regard to responsibility. The focus of attention will be on the law because it is in this context that we find the issues laid out explicitly and systematically.

Before preceding to a discussion of the correct analysis of coercion, it behooves us to examine more closely the prevalent, psychologically oriented view: Why won't it do?

There are several sorts of reasons why the "overpowered will" theory fails. In the first place, the law makes an exception that does not conform with the theory. Specifically, coercion is not recognized as an excuse for murder.[2] Yet given the credible threat of immediate death, the driver, as ordered, keeps going and does not stop or slow for the pedestrian crossing the street, killing him instantly. It would seem that the fear of his own death "overpowers" the driver's will. Why not be excused, then? But the law says, "Guilty." In common law as well as in many state statutes, coercion is no excuse for killing an innocent person.

Whatever one thinks of this rule in law, does it make sense if in fact the coerced victim's will is overcome, without power to act otherwise?

Another, perhaps more telling objection to the psychological analysis of coercion is the case of economic coercion. Such coercion is also a recognized excuse from responsibility in the law. There need be no "overwhelming" psychological "pressure." Thus in the leading case of *Young vs. Hoagland,* the court said, "[W]here by reason of the peculiar facts a reasonably prudent man finds that in order to preserve his property or protect his business interests it is necessary to make a payment of money which he does not owe and which in equity and in good conscience the receiver should not retain, he may recover it."[3]

Even more at odds with the "overborne will" theory of coercion is the classic legal doctrine in *Bram v. United States* concerning coerced confessions. *Bram* states that even a minimal influence, "however slight," that is imposed on a suspect in order to elicit a confession of guilt suffices in law to view that confession as coerced and to prohibit use of it against the person.[4]

Most fundamental, however, to the objection of the "overborne will" theory is the fact that there simply is no empirical evidence to back it up. No one has identified the "will," no one has observed it or measured it. No one even knows how to identify the point at which a person's will has "broken" or been "overpowered." Indeed it appears to many that it is more a term of metaphysics or theology than it is a genuine psychological entity.

Certainly we are not in these cases dealing with a "breakdown" such that there is no ability to will at all. Complete absence or non-functioning of the will would be the kind of thing we see in an epileptic seizure, or in tripping and falling, or, perhaps, in the body movements of a person asleep or unconscious.

It is true that in coercion, especially criminal coercion, we commonly observe that there is great fear. Yet in other cases of coercion there may be little sign of fear, merely of calculation. The tough-minded, crime-experienced, and fearless police officer who is threatened by a gun at the head may coolly comply, confident under the particular circumstances that compliance will end the matter. This is unquestionably criminal coercion, yet it is hard to imagine that the officer's will has been "broken."

Given this complete absence of empirical evidence for the theory, and given the types of cases acknowledged to be coercion that nevertheless exhibit little or no emotional fright or evidence of some psychologically "overwhelming" pressure, why would this theory find such near universal application in law and indeed in everyday life? It is, after all, ubiquitous in legal jargon, and plausible to the lay person.

In some way the language must make sense, must have some intuitive and powerful appeal. Wherein does this lie?

We might try to go right to the nub of the matter and say that by "overcome will" the law simply means "involuntary." Of course, as we have just seen, we could not mean "involuntary" in the sense that there is *no* will. Then, in what sense can one who acts *with* will be acting *in*voluntarily?

One thing that might be meant in law when one speaks of involuntary behavior is that the person is in some sense irrational. Sometimes the courts do speak of irrational behavior, for example, insane behavior, as involuntary. Of course, insanity is an excuse. But irrationality, whether in the form of insanity or any other legally recognized form, obviously does not fit the facts of the coercion case. Coerced behavior, even in the gun-at-the-head situation, is not irrational behavior. Quite to the contrary, such behavior is necessarily rational behavior. The coerced person knows what is to be done, why it is to be done, and then does it effectively in order to avoid the threatened action.

Perhaps the behavior is involuntary in the sense that the person is acting under some kind of "irresistible impulse." This is another kind of involuntariness that we run across in the law, though there is no consensus about the validity of such a concept. Existence of an irresistible impulse, if such could be proved, could indeed provide a legal ground for holding the act to be not voluntary. If proved in a case of coercion, it could provide a rationale for accepting coercion as a legal excuse.

There are difficulties with this approach, however. First of all, the notion of irresistible impulse is for theoretical purposes a very troublesome notion. The problem has been well expressed in the question: How do we tell the difference between "He could not resist his impulse" and "He did not resist his impulse"?[5] This becomes in practice a very perplexing issue in the law. Typically, when it comes up openly, as in insanity cases, for example, it involves psychiatric testimony. Yet there is no theoretical understanding of how to apply the distinction. What happens is that we get the expert testimony as to the facts about the defendant—facts about which there is commonly general agreement—and yet the experts disagree as to how to interpret the facts, and specifically whether the impulse, desire, or mood was irresistible or not. This, of course, is a pretty good sign that what we are dealing with here is not a question of fact, but a question of ideological differences among different schools of psychology and psychiatry.[6]

Most pertinent to the coercion defenses, however, is that when we deal with coercion defenses, we see that they generally call for little or no psychiatric testimony, and do not generate the typical problems and confusions of psychiatric testimony. This, again, is very good evidence that coercion in law does *not* raise an irresistible impulse type of issue, or indeed any psychological issues at all. Therefore, the involuntariness of coerced behavior is not to be understood along psychological lines.

A close cousin to the irresistible impulse is the notion of loss of self-control. If we assume that coercion must include loss of control, then indeed we might in law be on our way towards some kind of legal defense based on involuntariness. However, contrary to this assumption, we have to recognize that in the case of coercion the victim does not—and must not—lose self-control. Loss of self-control would entail inability to obey the coercer's orders, which in turn could trigger implementation of the threat.

Another psychological approach to getting at the meaning of coercion is the saying that when there is coercion the victim has no "real choice." Variants of this are that the victim had no "free choice," or had "no fair choice."

As far as "free choice" goes, the problem is that this term is more problematic than the one we want to explain, that is, "coercion." The notion of "freedom" has far more meanings, far more philosophical obscurities, and has generated far more controversy over the centuries than has the notion of coercion. As soon as one tries to link freedom with coercion, one finds that, rather than clarifying matters, one has introduced a whole new set of problems and controversies. Therefore the notion of no "free choice" is unhelpful in clarifying the notion of "coercion."

What about the idiom "no fair choice"? Here we have something that will be useful, especially with further refinement. If a criminal holds a gun at your head, threatens you, and orders you to help him, then you do not have a fair choice. A way of putting this in legal terms is that the person who coerces you has done something unlawful, that is, something "unfair" in a legally cognizable sense.

Not every lack of fair choice need arise out of coercion (it might have been deception, for example). However, every case of coercion would be an absence of fair choice—namely, an *unlawful* threat leaving no reasonable option but to comply.

But something odd has now happened. The crucial element is not mental but an external event—the coercer's unlawful threat. Instead of matters of psychology, we have to do with legal norms and the acts of others than the victim. This changes radically the focus of the legal inquiry from what the phrase "overcome the will" initially suggested.

Before pursuing this further, let us turn for still further insight to the last of the possibilities embodying the term "choice": the idea that where there is coercion, there is "no *real* choice." Obviously, this is a highly idiomatic approach. It certainly would not stand if taken literally; the coerced person does have a real choice in the obvious sense that the person could refuse to obey. Most writers on this topic agree that it is appropriate to describe the victim as someone who literally does make a choice. It may well be a deliberate choice, and indeed some people—more brave or more foolish than average—do indeed choose to resist. Yet there is plainly a certain appropriateness, idiomatically speaking, if one says, "I didn't really have a choice because he was holding a gun at my head." Our question must be: can we express plainly and more literally what this idiom tells us?

Specifically, we need to find a description of the facts in cases of coercion that is a true description, that shows why coercion properly negates responsibility, and that can with at least rough aptness be expressed in the idiom of the overborne will or the lack of choice.

I believe that what we are getting at here is the absence of a *reasonable* choice. Generally speaking, there is no reasonable choice if refusal means you immediately get your head blown off. One has the power to resist, but it is typically totally unreasonable to do so. If we allow this analysis of "no real choice" as a first approximation, we could make the transition plausibly from "coercion" to "no real choice," and thence to no reasonable alternative. There is nothing out of the ordinary here; the law often must rest on the concept of doing what is reasonable, that is, what the "reasonable" person would do.

Here again it turns out that nonvoluntariness is not a matter of some psychic process internal to the mind of the victim. Instead, the issue turns on the reasonableness of the choice to be made, a very different sort of issue indeed. The standards or canons of reasonableness can be quite objective, and in the legal context are typically taken to be so.

The matter can now be developed more positively and in detail by looking directly at the legal tests used for a criminal coercion defense. The classic test of criminal coercion is quite specific: there has to be a well-grounded or a credible threat of imminent death or serious injury for failure to obey the coercer's demand. As mentioned earlier, English and American law have historically treated coercion as a defense to any criminal charge except murder.

Of course, a person who is in a spot like this might very well experience great inner turmoil—not a breakdown, but intense emotion. This, however, is not essential for coercion. The test in question asks nothing about the victim's emotional state, unlike what is suggested by the looser ancillary commentary of judges about a broken will. The test does not require that one show loss of self-control or irresistible impulse. The defense requires no proof of intense fear or panic. The legal test in effect eliminates psychology entirely. We remain with questions of reasonableness and questions of lawfulness as these are interpreted in legal terms.

We can now test this approach for its generalizability by turning to coercion in a different area of the law, the area of coerced confessions. In the area of coerced confessions, the legal tests of coercion differ markedly from those used in a criminal coercion defense. Making a confession is not a criminal act at all. Instead we have a question of doing something under coercion that is lawful but damaging to one's interests. The claim of coercion is a claim that the confession ought not to be admitted in evidence because it was not voluntary.

The classic legal tests here are specific and are adapted to this special type of circumstance. The *Bram* test, which still dominates doctrine in this area, was a late nineteenth-century case. In substance, it specifies that if the person confessed because of any kind of threat or promise or *any* improper influence whatsoever, then the confession was coerced[7]—and the person coerced should not be held legally responsible for what was said in the "confession," which is to say that the confession should be inadmissible in evidence.

Here, then, we have the other extreme from the criminal defense, for the criminal defense of coercion requires a mortal threat. When one thinks of that paradigmatic gun-at-the-head situation, it is plausible to think of a "will overcome." But the *Bram* test merely requires any kind of improper influence, no matter how slight. Here it is no longer plausible to talk about overcoming or destroying the will or subverting the will. And yet the surprising thing is that the courts still use this traditional rhetoric, derived from the premodern cases of torture-induced confessions. In modern confession cases, torture is seldom at issue.

In the famous *Culombe* case, for example, Justice Frankfurter spoke of a "drained capacity for free choice"[8] by use of "subtler devices" than "ropes and a rubber hose."[9] What were the facts? The police asked his wife and children to visit Culombe in the jail, and the police encouraged them to appeal to him to confess.

Culombe was a person of low intelligence, but he knew what he was doing. He had consistently refused to confess, but his family talked to him and persuaded him that he ought to confess. So he decided to confess, and did so, giving appropriate reasons and thereafter consistently affirming these. This does not at all fit the model suggested by the language of the will overcome, destroyed, neutralized, subverted, or even "drained."

Why, then, do the courts continue to use the dramatic rhetoric of the broken will here? The answer is probably along the lines suggested by Justice Frankfurter's words. It is quite evident that the evil to be corrected is the improper use of state power by police officers to oppress an individual who is at least temporarily under their influence. Historically, the reality was torture. Basic constitutional principles of individual liberty and of restraint on state oppression have made it appropriate to impose strict constraints on police power here. So even mild impropriety, if it could have any influence on something so important as a confession to crime, is impermissible.

Yet when the specific concept of "coercion" is used as the key concept element in the legal rationale, the courts speak in the ways traditional in legal precedent.

Nowadays the "improper influences" are often nothing at all like torture; the courts have had to explain away the implausibility of their idiom by speaking of "subtler" forms of pressure. Thus the necessary legal rhetoric is used, but it has lost its sense. (And indeed the tendency has recently been to invoke explicit rules excluding such confessions rather than to argue in terms of "coercion.")

We can now shift to another, very different area of law, the area of so-called economic or business law, and the legal notion of "economic coercion." Here again, the legal criteria of coercion differ substantially from those of criminal or confession coercion. Consider the case of a railroad company subject to a tax that it thinks is unconstitutionally being imposed upon it.[10] The company does not want to pay the tax. On the other hand, the tax law has an automatic trigger penalty provision, such that if they do not pay the tax properly and on time, they will in effect be shut down instantly. This would of course cause a major economic loss to them. So they pay under protest, and then they sue for redress, that is, for return of the tax money, on the ground that they had paid under coercion. The court agrees that it was an unconstitutionally imposed tax, and therefore the company had been unlawfully threatened. The court also finds that the company had no reasonable alternative, that it could never have obtained suitable redress if the railroad had been shut down for refusal to pay at once. Thus, since the company was unlawfully deprived of any reasonable alternative but to pay, the payment was coerced.

Notice once again that the crucial issues are "objective"—legal and economic. The threat was unconstitutional; the reasonableness of the alternatives was calculable in terms of profit, loss, and procedures for legal redress. Thus, we again have eliminated the psychological element entirely from the concept of coercion here. Moreover, we are dealing with corporations, impersonal (nonpsychological) entities. The psychology of the executives who are involved is totally irrelevant. If in fact the president of the company were afraid of something, this would be legally totally irrelevant. Yet, if one looks at the text of this and other such cases, one finds that the familiar psychological imagery is used. The courts speak of the company being "compelled to yield."

Individuals can also be subject to economic duress, for example, when an employee is threatened with being fired by his employer for refusal to sign a waiver.[11] The employee may indeed be frightened and worried. And the courts will always mention this sort of thing, because it does fit the traditional rhetoric of coercion. But even if the employee were cool and calculating about it, it still would be economic coercion if he were unlawfully threatened in such a way that the only reasonable thing to do was to agree. And it remains ultimately a legal question, for the court to decide, whether the options were or were not reasonable.

Conclusion: The Rationale for Excusing in Case of Coercion

We are now prepared to ask and answer the question: Given that all the elements of a specific act as legally defined are present, why should a victim of coercion be relieved of the burdens normally entailed? The answer is quite simple and direct: It is true by legal definition that where there is coercion, the victim is an innocent, wronged party. Moreover, the victim acted reasonably under the circumstances. Finally, the coercer is acting wrongly and is inducing the victim to act as he or she otherwise would not. It is the very essence of law—it is the *raison d'être* of the law—to protect and defend those who are innocent and who act reasonably. Punitive sanctions should be imposed on the wrongdoer, not the innocent, reasonable person. This simple and intuitive rationale consists in an objective rather than psychological, subjective formula.

Although not discussed here, the same basic formula is applicable to the traditional forms of legal claims under rubrics such as duress and undue influence. *Mutatis mutandis*, the same holds for coercion in nonlegal contexts where coercion entails excuse from responsibility for the coerced person's actions or the burdens normally consequent upon those actions.

Self-Deception

Introduction

Self-deception is one of the favored means of evading, or trying to evade, responsibility. Yet the notion of self-deception has posed a nagging puzzle. How can one successfully lie to oneself? How can one believe what one knows to be false? Such notions seem like blatant self-contradictions.

Yet people do deceive themselves. They do (try to) evade responsibility by doing this, and there is a certain sincerity in manifesting the false belief. Not surprisingly, the concept of self-deception has been the starting point for many philosophical inquiries.[*] A number of different efforts have been made to resolve the puzzle.

What follows is the argument that these discussions have been fundamentally misguided. Their premise has been the usual one—that the concept of self-deception poses a puzzle. That premise is wrong. The source of the puzzlement is not the concept of self-deception. Self-deception needs no explaining. The aura of paradox has its source in the failure to appreciate properly how our mind ordinarily and normally works. If we have a proper appreciation of how the mind works, the concept of self-deception loses its problematic character.

This is a revised version of "Self-Deception Needs No Explaining," *Philosophical Quarterly* 48, no. 192 (1998): 289–300.
[*]See the appendix at the end of this chapter.

In order to see the truth of the preceding claims, we need first to consider some of the ways in which the mind normally works when we are conscious.

How the Mind Works

As I sit here writing, I am conscious of the thoughts I am at this moment embodying in pen and ink on paper. Or, to use the specific language I find useful for further discussion, my attention is focused on my thoughts at the moment. It is also focused on the words as they appear physically on the paper. Of course, I am holding the pen in a special grip, the grip I habitually use in writing with pen and ink. However, my attention is not focused on the position of my fingers around the pen—or at least it was not until just now when I began to think and write about the grip. In any case, it is rare that I focus attention upon the grip. I use it, time and time again, skillfully, but as I would say, "without thinking." It is "habit."

The word "habit" should not obscure the fact that my fingers move the pen in ever-changing, subtly differentiated ways to shape the letters and lines on the page that express my thoughts. This is not "habit" in the sense of a mechanical, repetitive motion; it is not an autonomous motion that, once triggered, goes its programmed way. The obvious fact is that in moving the pen I take account not only of the words in which I wish to express my thoughts, but also of the movements required for legible writing, and the relation of the pen to the borders of the page and to the invisible horizontal line of the writing. I adapt continuously to all of this and more "without thinking," "subconsciously," "unconsciously"—by which I mean that I am not focusing my attention on it.

Am I somehow aware of these arm, hand, and finger movements, and the conditions to which they respond? One could say that I am normally unaware of all this. On the other hand, if I were to keep writing on the same line even after I reached the right-hand edge of the paper, or if I drifted significantly off the horizontal, someone might properly say, "You're not paying attention to what you're doing." And so I would correct this by turning more of my attention to the writing in relation to the paper's edges and the line of writing. "More attention" than what? Obviously, more than before—which is to recognize that while I was focusing my attention on my thoughts and the words needed to express them, I was nevertheless taking account of where my pen was on the page and how it moved. I spelled correctly, but my attention was not focused on this. I used correct grammar in a flexible way, adapted to my thought, but I was not directing my attention to the rules of grammar.

For the sake of convenience and clarity, I shall express the matter in this way: when I am writing as I normally do, I take account of the complex and varying physical and linguistic requirements for putting my thoughts on paper, but I do not focus my attention on these things. Yet I do all this purposely, intelligently, and adaptively. The crux of the matter, then, is that we can take intelligent account of something in our mental or physical environment, and respond in an intelligently adaptive way, without having to focus our attention on it.

An important consequence of my taking account of things upon which I do not focus my attention is that usually I cannot later describe the details of what went on in that peripheral region of my awareness. Often I have no recollection of it at all. Thus when I later read a printed copy of what I have written, I may remember when and where I wrote it, remember what I wrote, yet have little or no recollection of the particular finger and arm motions I made at any particular place on the page. Of course, it takes training and learning to be able to write without having to focus attention on the doing of it. But that is precisely what it is to learn to write with reasonable fluency.

The nature of this mental capacity bears further elaboration in order to make explicit how complex and sophisticated is the exercise of it. While I am writing, there are the noises of passing cars, the neighbor's lawnmower, the kitchen refrigerator, all coming to my ears. They are irrelevant to my writing, indeed, would disrupt it were I to focus my attention on them. The fact is, I am simply unconscious of the noises. How can this be? The noises certainly register in my ears. It has to be that I take account of them, recognize their irrelevance to my project at the moment, and therefore do not turn my attention to the noises—nor do I even focus attention on the fact that I am doing this.

Do I really do something as complex as evaluating the relevance of each noise? That I do so is illustrated by the following mundane situation. In the midst of writing, I hear my wife's car as it comes down our driveway. Of all the noises I'm hearing, I single this one out. It's the signal that my wife has arrived home. I want to greet her when she comes in, and in this case I also want to deliver several messages left for her. I have recognized that noise as relevant to my current interests. So I now direct my attention primarily to her and away from the writing.

I do all this "in the back of my mind," that is, without having turned my attention to the fact that I am doing it. Without focusing my attention on what I am doing, I nevertheless actively direct and redirect my attention for what I consider are good and sufficient reasons.

It bears emphasis that not only was there an absence of any reason earlier to focus my attention on the car noises, but there was also a good reason to avoid turning my attention to them. I took account of the fact that the noises were irrelevant to my writing, and therefore would disturb my writing. Thus, I intentionally resist turning attention to the noises, and I also avoid turning my attention to the fact that I am doing so. As a result, both the noises and my attitude towards them are outside the field of my attention.

All these things are so familiar and obvious as to seem hardly to justify the lengths to which I have gone to call them to attention. Yet in the matter of intelligently guided responsiveness without focused attention, I have as yet barely scratched the surface.

For example, in order for my words to make sense they must fit the context. I have to take into account what I wrote in the previous paragraph. In a less detailed way I also have to take into account all that I have written up to this point, as well as the direction I wish the argument to take. Beyond this I have to take into account a vast and complex background—the philosophical sources and ideas that inspire my project, the canons of style that govern my writing, the anticipated response of readers to my language and my ideas, and much more. Failure to take such considerations into account as I write will produce blunders, inconsistencies, confusion, stylistic awkwardness. Yet very few, if any of these, are at the center of my attention.

The very fact that confusions or blunders do occasionally appear shows that the rest of the time I am effectively taking all this context into account "without thinking." It is only because this is so that the ideas and writing on which I am now concentrating my attention do turn out, by and large, to be consistent with what I have written in the paragraphs and pages above and consistent with my beliefs, attitudes, and general information.

On a number of occasions I have been driving home from work while brooding about some problem at the office—only to arrive home and suddenly realize that I have no recollection of the drive itself. I believe this to be a fairly common experience for us all. Indeed, I recently had a more remarkable version of this experience. The route I was driving was one rarely traveled by me, and it was quite complicated. Because my attention was focused on a lively discussion we were having in the car, when I arrived home I had no memory whatsoever of having driven that route. Such experiences dramatize our normal and generally unremarked capacity to carry out intelligently, in the background of our mind, projects of complexity and substantial duration, while directing our attention elsewhere.

This human capacity to act intelligently within a context vastly too complex to be given attention all at once is surely incomparably more developed in us than in any other species. It is an amazingly efficient capacity exercised all day, every day, every minute of the day. Its advantage in the evolutionary scheme of things is self-evident. It is a mark of the distinctively human form of intelligence.

Such, then, in brief, is the relevant natural history of the mind at work.

Self-Deception

What makes self-deception seem puzzling is a misconception of the nature of this normal mental activity. The error consists in assuming that when we take account of anything and respond intelligently, we must focus our attention on what we are doing.

This assumption is false. The focus of attention is motivated. Usually it is motivated in part by what is at the center of our attention. But it is always also motivated by circumstances of which we are aware but which are outside the focus of our attention.

Assume that one is aware of something that has a distressing or even traumatic significance. A shameful or guilty impulse, an embarrassing act, a blow to one's self-esteem—these are all the more painful when one focuses one's attention on them. Avoidance or minimizing of such pain is therefore a powerful motive to refrain from focusing attention on them. I can do this just as I can refrain from focusing my attention on the noise of passing cars. In each case I have a strong motive to do this. I do it without paying attention to what I am doing, thus avoiding distraction from the effort to keep attention away from the car noises, or avoiding the feeling of guilt were I to attend to my evasive maneuvering.

It bears emphasis that there is no special mental trick in this. It is simply a case of doing what I always do: I focus attention where I have reason to think it will be profitable, or pleasing, or necessary to do so. I avoid focusing attention on that which I take to be irrelevant, distracting, or unavoidably painful. Where these motives conflict, I strike what seems the desirable balance—without the need to focus my attention on this activity.

The self-deceiver often seeks to disguise the deception with an alibi or prejudicial account of what actually happened. Suppose, for example, that I have done something shameful. Just because this particular shame is deeply wounding to me, I avoid focusing my attention on what I did. However, events or challenges by others may force the memory of it to the fore. In that case I may try to escape the pain by claiming nobler motives than I actually had. Or I may describe the occasion in a way that would make it innocent. Perhaps I insist that I didn't say what others say I said. Or I insist that what I said was intended in jest, or as an exclamation to be understood as preposterous.

In short, I avert my attention from that aspect of my action that was shameful. Instead, I focus my attention on the plausibility of my overt account of the matter. Thus there is a certain element of sincerity in what I claim to be true.

I pay a price for this. I lose the opportunity to appraise my conduct realistically by paying close attention to it. I have less reliable recall, and can thus more readily rationalize what happened. I shall be less creative and less subtle about handling the matter. Perhaps most important, I lose the (painful) chance of acquiring self-knowledge.

Of course, in spite of my attempts to avoid turning my attention to the shameful aspect of my conduct, I may be taken by surprise when unexpected evidence of my shameful act comes to light. Though I may offer an alibi, I may at least initially seem shifty or flustered, awkward, or simply not believable. From such tell-tale signs the close observer may say of me that "in his heart" he secretly does know how shameful the act was.

And indeed I secretly do know. But since I avoid focusing my attention on it, it is in a way a secret even from myself.

Lest we be over-puritanical, we should recognize that there can be situations in which the burden of assuming responsibility for one's actions is beyond one's power to bear. Others may legitimately hold us responsible. But we ourselves take cover in self-deception. Orestes murders his mother. He is aghast at the crime. But then he cries out that it was the god who told him to commit this terrible crime.

The Arts: A Variant Form of Self-Deception

Since the preceding analysis of the mind's working may be unfamiliar, it may help to explore a related but very familiar area. The arts provide a model closely related to that of self-deception. The gap between reality in the world of the drama and the reality of our everyday practical world is a case in point.

We know that the actors are not engaged in spontaneous conversations, that the lines are memorized and repeated nightly by rote. We know this is not Othello, nor is the woman's name really Desdemona. It is all sham. Yet we continuously avoid paying attention to the sham. It is an attitude we adopt spontaneously when the curtain goes up. We turn our attention to the story rather than the otherwise obvious sham aspect. We avert our attention from the people sitting around us, from the general theater setting. We are immersed in the story world. We react with genuine emotions that are intelligible in the context of the drama. They are not intelligible as reactions to our being seated in a theatre. We are truly, deeply moved. There is a certain genuineness and sincerity. It is not pretense.

Yet, on the other hand, there is something fictional about the emotion. The emotions we experience in the world of the drama are not identical to the emotional reactions of our everyday world. We do not cry out in anger at Othello, nor do we rush to the stage to protect Desdemona when she is attacked. At the periphery of our attention we are aware of the "real world" context. We sit quietly, even as we sincerely grieve over the murder of this innocent victim.

This is the pattern of response we also see in self-deception. It is a form of sincerity, of authentic belief and emotional reaction. To insist that one must either believe or not believe the dramatic or the self-deceptive story, that one cannot have both at the same time, is to create an unnecessary puzzle.

Similar comments could be made about literature and the visual arts. We often react powerfully, yet we have no impulse to reach for and eat Cézanne's wonderful apples. We experience a variety of strong emotions when reading of Jane Austen's heroine Anne Elliot, but we do not seek to learn her date of death.

The mental process in self-deception is the same as in the "suspension of disbelief" in the arts. However, the motives in the latter case and the quality of the experience are profoundly different from those in self-deception.

Conclusion

In the preceding remarks my theses hover in the neighborhood of such depth psychology notions as "conscious," "unconscious," "repression," "subconscious," "defensive." I have at times used some of these words, but only in a nontechnical sense. It is essential to my method that I have used only everyday language in describing how the mind works. However this study does throw some light on these notions, though I will not pursue the matter here.

Nor do I pursue here the morality or practical value of self-deception. These questions are important, and they merit deeper inquiry. I have merely noted without argument that at times deceiving oneself may be psychologically necessary if one is to avoid being overcome by unbearable suffering.

The object of this chapter has been limited to showing that self-deception entails no special, aberrant, or otherwise distinctive mental maneuvers. It is a normal mental maneuver with the distinctive aim of covertly avoiding acceptance of responsibility by means of deceiving oneself.

APPENDIX
Works on Self-Deception

It would be otiose to list here a full bibliography of the very large philosophical literature on self-deception. However what follows is an abbreviated list of citations to some of the earlier influential books, collections, and individual articles that established the debate about the supposed paradox of self-deception.

Canfield, John V., and Donald F. Gustafson. "Self Deception." *Analysis* 23 (1962): 32–36.

Chisholm, Roderick, and Thomas D. Feehan. "The Intent to Deceive." *Journal of Philosophy* 74 (1977):143–59.

Demos, Raphael. "Lying to Oneself." *Journal of Philosophy* 57 (1960): 588–95.

Fingarette, Herbert. *Self-Deception*. London: Routledge and Kegan Paul, 1969.

Foss, Jeffery. "Rethinking Self-Deception." *American Philosophical Quarterly* 17 (1980): 237–43.

Haight, M. R. *A Study of Self-Deception*. Sussex: The Harvester Press, 1980.

Hamlyn, D. W. "Self Deception." *Proceedings of the Aristotelian Society*, supp. vol. 45 (1971): 45–60.

Martin, Mike W., ed. *Self-Deception and Self-Understanding: New Essays in Philosophy and Psychology*. Lawrence: University Press of Kansas, 1985.

McLaughlin, Brian P., and Amélie Oksenberg Rorty, eds. *Perspectives on Self-Deception*. Berkeley and Los Angeles: University of California Press, 1988.

Mounce, H. O. "Self-Deception." *Proceedings of the Aristotelian Society*, supp. vol. 45 (1971): 61–72.

Paluch, Stanley. "Self-Deception." *Inquiry* 10 (1967): 268–78.

Pears, David. "Self-Deceptive Belief Formation." *Synthèse* 89 (1991): 393–405.

Penelhum, Terence. "Pleasure and Falsity." In *Philosophy of Mind*, edited by Stuart Hampshire, 242–60. New York: Harper & Row, 1966.

Pugmire, David. "'Strong' Self-Deception." *Inquiry* 12 (1969): 339–46.

Sartre, Jean-Paul. "Bad Faith." In *Being and Nothingness*, translated by Hazel E. Barnes, chap. 2. New York: Philosophical Library, 1956.

Saunders, John Turk. "The Paradox of Self-Deception." *Philosophy and Phenomenological Research* 35 (1975): 559–70.

Siegler, Frederick A. "Self-Deception and Other-Deception." *Journal of Philosophy* 60 (1963): 759–64.

Szabados, Bela. "Self-Deception." *Canadian Journal of Philosophy* 4 (1974): 51–68.

The Hindu Perspective:
The Bhagavad Gita

"What is action? What is nonaction? As to this [says Krishna] even the sages are perplexed."[1]

To be wise, says Krishna, one must see "action in inaction, and inaction in action."[2]

My aim here is to present some philosophical reflections on this paradox. Specifically, I want to propose a way of seeing its truth directly, and of explaining it conceptually.

There are, of course, a number of well-known passages and themes in the Bhagavad Gita that can be seen as explaining what "actionless action" means.[3] The interpretation I offer is not one of those explicit in the Gita. As a philosopher inspired by the text, rather than as an expert on the text, I offer my own interpretation because I believe not only that it works well as an interpretation of the language of the Gita, but also that it can be seen to be true and thus lends a credibility beyond that of dogma or authority to this profoundly important but paradoxical doctrine. Though I do not have space to do so here, I would also argue that familiar doctrines in the Gita, doctrines closely related to actionless action, can be logically derived from the interpretation I offer here.[4]

This is a revised version of "Action and Suffering in the Bhagavad Gita," *Philosophy East and West* 34, no. 4 (1984): 357–69.

Later I will present a more rigorous analysis, but I will begin with an impressionistic and "phenomenological" discussion.

Think of those awakenings out of sleep in the dark hours of morning. One is unable to get back to sleep; one's mind races. This situation can be described in two contrasting ways. It can be viewed as my passivity, my-being-acted-upon, thoughts imposing themselves on me. Or it can equally well be seen as a form of action, of me-as-acting, me as the thinker. From the passive perspective, thoughts enter my mind; they race through it. They force themselves on me; I cannot control them. From the active perspective I wake up, and I start thinking gloomy thoughts. Why do I do this? Perverse of me! But I do it. These are my thoughts, thoughts I think; this is what I am doing.

The experience of racing thoughts in the middle of the night is a dramatic example, a very special case. What about more ordinary cases of everyday mental activity? Do they also show this double aspect?

For example, as I first wrote these words I was thinking, and writing down what I was thinking. This is for me—far more than most of my thinking—the kind of thinking that is carried on in an orderly, rational, disciplined way. It seems at the opposite pole from my madly racing tangle of night thoughts. It seems the very model of the active rather than the passive.

Yet I can equally well view it in the passive mode, and describe it accordingly: As I sat at my desk, thoughts arose in my mind—and fortunately they arose in what turned out to be a certain orderly sequence, as I desired would be the case. But in spite of that desire, as happens all too often, the thoughts might have arisen in a less orderly way, even in a confused pattern disrupted by the emergence of irrelevant thoughts.

What do I do in order that an orderly sequence of thoughts should occur? The answer is: I sit myself at the desk, with writing materials, and I resolve, or decide, or adopt the intention, to think further about these philosophical issues and to write down my thoughts. Thereupon thoughts emerge. But how did just the right thought pop into my mind at that right moment? How did I do it? I certainly did not have the thought "beforehand," ready and waiting; and even if I had, it certainly was not there always. This would be an endless regression. There has to be a point where the thought is not yet being thought, but (fortunately), just when I need it, it pops up in my mind.

The question reemerges: How did I manage that a thought that I did not have in mind a moment before should suddenly and in a timely way happen to come to me? And how is it that, if I continue to be fortunate, further thoughts pop into my mind in an orderly way? Here is rational thinking at its most orderly—and yet, it happens, or all too often it does not happen. I must be patient—the word "patient" means, of course, passive. Thus my most disciplined, controlled thinking is, as seen from another angle, something that happens to me, in me. I am actively thinking; but at the heart of that activity is passivity.

So much for rationally disciplined thought—but what of the "creative" imagination? It is a platitude that even the most creative mind, however hard working, must in the end wait for the Muse to speak, wait for the new idea to be born, hope that it will happen. Creative thinking and doing—the archetype of activity—has its deep core of passivity.

What I have said can be generalized to apply to mental activities of all kinds—to remembering, hoping, fearing, enjoying, dis-enjoying, longing, loving, imagining, contemplating. . . . For example, memories come to me when I "summon them up." That is, I remember things. Yet memories don't always come when I summon them up. I set myself to recall something, but have to wait to see if it comes to mind. I must wait to see. I am passive in this regard—yet I am active, I am recalling.

There are times when I would maintain hope, but hope does not stay; or I attempt to cast away hope—yet it remains in spite of me. It seems I am passive. Yet it is, after all, I who hope—so I am active.

Finally, and most central to the phenomena in question, because it bears so directly on all action, whether bodily or mental, is the element of purpose and the execution of purpose. My purpose is my actively intending, willing, directing of my activity. Purpose lies at the very core of myself as active. And—like my thoughts and memories—purposes come to me. I might even say they come upon me. I can think, hope, wish, expect, resolve that on a certain occasion it will be my effective purpose to act with generosity. But will such be my purpose when I confront the moment? Perhaps, perhaps not. At times I surprise myself. I must, in the end, wait to see what purpose comes to mind and establishes itself as my purpose. Sad to say, I at times discover when the issue is joined that my purpose is a selfish one. Yet, it is my purpose, what I propose to do. Purposing, too, has its active and passive aspects.

It is time now to turn from impressionistic characterization, and to formulate explicitly the nature of the inaction in action.

The words "act," "action," and "actualize" have the same root—to actualize, says the *Oxford English Dictionary,* is to realize in action. Action is purposefully making something happen as one intends, the realizing or actualizing of purpose. When something takes place that is not purposed, it is a happening, even if it be the motion of my body; it is no action.[5]

When I speak of purpose I am interested in what I call executive purpose[6]—the point being that mere wishing or planning, mere antecedent intentions, are not what I mean. In the concept of executive purpose it is by definition necessary that there be movement toward actualizing the purpose, even though final success or consummation of the act is not necessary. Thus, as I shall use the words here, "purpose" and "action" are inextricable. Where there is executive purpose there is at least incipient action; and where there is action—as distinguished from mere accidental or unintentional behavior—there is necessarily executive purpose. One could speak here of "intention" or even of the "will." But these notions are now so fraught with built-in assumptions, so laden with theories, confusions, and ambiguities arising out of centuries of conflicting philosophical theories, that I prefer to use more neutral language.

My most immediate executive purpose at this moment is to write these very words, which I do by making this sequence of marks on paper. This purpose is of course an integral, subsidiary element in executing a larger executive purpose of mine—to express and communicate to others some of my thoughts about the concept of actionless action.

Insofar as my executive purposes are being successfully executed, I am controlling affairs, I am exercising power over them, I am acting effectively. That is what we mean by exercising power or control over affairs. But things may go contrary to my executive purpose—the pen runs out of ink, my vision blurs. Or I do manage to write the words, but they do not well capture or communicate my larger thought. Or those thoughts are in themselves well expressed but they turn out to lead into a tangle of philosophical problems or confusions. Insofar as my executive purpose is frustrated, I am losing control, my power is ineffective. I experience it consciously as less and less a question of what I am doing, more and more as what is happening to me. I see myself as the patient rather than the agent. (Of course it is I who am thinking the now blundering thoughts.)

There remains a third paradigmatic possibility in addition to purpose effected and purpose frustrated. Things may go along in the absence of any relevant purpose of mine. I hear a siren whine outside, I see that night falls, I dimly sense my heart beating. Here I am not controlling. They are happening; yet neither am I failing to control, mis-controlling, or being ineffectual and frustrated. Not all that happens to me represents miscarried purpose. What, then, is the general concept, what is the word I need here to characterize that which happens to or in me, in contrast to that which I myself do, my actions? "Experiencing" is too broad, for I also experience what I purposively do, such as writing.

The word "undergoing" is in the right neighborhood. Or I could say these things "affect" me, or are "happening" to me, or in me, or around me. The words will work in some contexts but in others are idiomatically out of place. In truth we do not have a modern, commonly used English word to express precisely the important concept that is at issue here—the exact contrary of "to act."

There is, however, an English word that in its derivation from Greek and Latin, in its classical English use, and in contemporary literary or formal use, can express the concept exactly. That word is "to suffer." In its generic sense, it is the exact antonym of "to act." "To suffer" is rendered in the dictionary as "to undergo," to "bear under," to "be affected by," to "endure," to "let happen." "Suffer the little children to come unto me" has no connotation of distress. It simply means "Let them come" (German: "Lasset die Kindlein zu mir kommen"). But of course in modern English the common usage is narrower. The word "suffer" usually means not merely to undergo but, more specifically, to undergo pain, distress, or misery. The specific connotation of misery, now ubiquitous in common speech, obscures the more general and fundamental concept, that of simply being affected by something or in some way.

It is no accident that "to suffer" should take on as a dominant meaning "to suffer misery." It is because, as the Gita tells us, we are in bondage to karman (action). We strive to impose our own purposes on the world. The result of this ubiquitous disposition is that to suffer, to be acted on rather than to be the actor, is perforce to be disappointed, frustrated, defeated, pained. Thus the word "suffer" comes in practice to signify "suffer misery."[7]

This point does not rest on an accident of language. The generic English sense of "suffer" is not peculiar to the English language. As the *Oxford English Dictionary* reports, the Latin origin of "suffer" also has the generic sense—"to bear under." The Greek word *paschein* and related words such as *pathetikos* and *pathetos* express the same generic concept of letting happen, of being affected by or receptive to what happens.[8] The Greek is, of course, the source of such English words as "patient," "passion," "passive," which in their classical English meanings—as in "the patience of Job"[9]—also have the sense of "suffer" in the generic sense that is the antonym of action.[10] It is interesting that in modern English usage the words "passion" or "passivity" have come to reflect our background commitment to purposively controlling our life. "Passion" then comes to mean not merely something undergone, something that overcomes one, but something active, even aggressive.

The truth, of course—as Arjuna and Job came to appreciate—is that suffering need not mean weakness or misery. It can equally well signify the contrary.

One paradigmatic form of beatific suffering is the experience of full surrender to a masterwork of music. The movement of mind and spirit is then totally controlled by the music. Our personal purposes, external to the music, have simply disappeared from consciousness. Here perfect suffering is the condition of perfect participation—and if the music is sublime or joyful, we participate in that sublimity or joy.[11] As for weakness versus strength—at least in the classic texts—the powers of enlightened sufferers such as Arjuna and Job are both multiplied and enhanced.

We should take account, too, of the complex form of suffering that could be called mis-action or mal-action, failed or faulty action, the miscarriage of purpose.

We now have entrée into the threefold distinction propounded in the Gita by Krishna. Having said that action and nonaction puzzle even the sages,[12] he goes on to say, "Of action there must be understanding, of mal-action there must be understanding, of non-action there must be understanding—the path of action goes deep and is hard to see."[13]

We are now prepared to see the truth of Krishna's central message: The deepest wisdom is to see "the action in inaction, and inaction in action." In this perspective, says Krishna, I am confused if I contemplate my doing something and say of that event: "I am the doer."[14] The truth is that, from the wider viewpoint, I also see that "I am not the doer."[15]

Where, when, and how often do initiating purposes emerge? The answer, in the end, is sweeping in character. Executive purpose is always, at least in some significant aspect, an initial purpose. Indeed it is so in at least the following two respects.

The first step toward seeing this is to recall that actions characteristically come under a hierarchy of increasingly general purposes. The more general and inclusive a purpose is, the more indeterminate it is. Subsidiary purposes are relatively specific and determinate. For example, my purpose in writing this is to present an analysis of the Gita. This purpose is a rather inclusive executive purpose, which is to say that it leaves open what particular words I will use. In contrast, my specific purpose at this moment is to write these very words as part of that analysis. As such it was not specifically determined by my larger purpose.

The larger purpose of writing this essay must itself have arisen at some point as initial purpose. It did so as subsidiary to some still larger purpose—perhaps writing a book. Or my purpose of writing this essay may have emerged as the origin de novo of a hierarchy and sequence of purposes.

The second respect in which all purpose is initial has to do with the dynamic aspect of purpose. My purpose in writing these very words is subsidiary to my larger purpose of writing the essay. But in writing these words I reaffirm my larger purpose, for it is always possible for me to abandon the larger purpose because of dissatisfaction with what I am writing.

Thus each subsidiary purpose is not only an initial one in regard to its specific content, it is also (as Sartre so powerfully argued) a fundamentally de novo reaffirmation of the larger purpose.

In summary, then, it is both experientially and conceptually apparent that each and every action is also nonaction. What is action when viewed as the execution of purpose is nonaction when viewed as arising out of initial purpose, purpose that simply comes upon me and is not determined by any prior purpose of mine.

It must be emphasized that to say a purpose is an initial or de novo purpose is not to say that it is uncaused; nor is it to say that it was caused. An initial purpose is an un-purposed purpose; it may or may not be caused by something other than a prior purpose. This issue merits further comment here.

In the Gita, causation of purpose is very much emphasized. Krishna alludes to at least two major kinds of causal influences that are not themselves purposes but that contribute to the formation of purposes. One sort of influence is that of the three *gunas*.[16] The *gunas* are the three basic impulses in nature that are generally supposed to govern human conduct. They are *sattva* (truth, purity), *rajas* (passion, energy), and *tamas* (darkness, sloth). Another sort of influence is karmic influence, the influence of one's past action on present action.[17] Both are natural influences that play an enormous role in shaping my present purpose and hence present action. As Krishna says, "Nature acts; only the confused think 'I am the doer.'"[18]

On the other hand, the existence of some genuine initiative on Arjuna's part is strongly suggested by the fact that the central dramatic point of the Gita narrative is for Krishna to persuade Arjuna to change his purpose and his conduct.[19] Krishna's appeals would be pointless if Arjuna's destiny were not in some basic respect open to an authentic initiative by Arjuna.

The Gita does not state clearly what the exact relationships are when it comes to the causal influences on Arjuna's purposes and the power of Arjuna genuinely to initiate. I offer no answers here. It is more important at this point to appreciate that the Gita bypasses, and in an important sense undercuts, the traditional Western preoccupation with free will and determinism. It is not that the Gita declares one side or the other in the debate to be wrong. Instead the Gita's teaching implies that the very preoccupation with the question arises out of delusion.

More specifically, the central delusion (*moha*) arises from erroneously adopting the perspective of action as of ultimate significance, rather than adopting the truly ultimate perspective, which is that of suffering. It is the focus on action, on the individual as actor, that leads naturally to the whole cluster of familiar ideas associated with the free will debate. These include the idea of the individual's moral responsibility, and the related ideas of personal guilt, remorse, retributive blame, punishment, and reward as personal desert. These notions are designed to make sense of a world in which the actor's purposeful initiative is seen as centrally meaningful.

The gist of my analysis of the Gita, however, is that, whatever the sources of our purposes and action, it matters not. They may in some respects be entirely determined by the *gunas*. They may be determined by our past *karman* or by anything else. They may in some respects be of genuinely de novo origin in the self. For in any case, no matter which one or combination of these assumptions be made, it would still be that the emergence of initial purpose is something I do not control. For initial purpose is not brought into being as the execution of some prior purpose.[20] Thus it is my role as sufferer, and not as actor, that is of deepest and widest significance.

Of course, each actor is unique, and make a unique contribution. The uniqueness of each actor's contribution does not signify, however, that the actor is the "author" of the act,[21] that is, its ultimate controller-creator. This view of the actor as author arises out of confusion rooted in a misplaced emphasis. It gives rise to the notions of personal responsibility and of free will. When matters are correctly and fully in focus, the individual as actor is not the author of meaning. Our world vision changes and the world order and its maintenance[22] become the central—the epic—drama. In it, we actors play with some spontaneity our roles as written in the script provided by history.

The generic concept of suffering defines the inner unity that binds the two possible conditions of human existence—bondage and liberation. Both bondage and liberation are forms of suffering. The spiritual crisis posed in the Gita is not—as it can easily seem—the option between suffering and no-suffering. The true alternatives are two different ways of suffering. A person who is attached to the objects of personal desire, who strives for the execution of personal purposes, suffers the miserable and mind-distracting frustrations of the deluded.[23] On the other hand, even if we do act with attachment, we are no more sufferers than if we act without attachment. In the latter case it is a different kind of suffering.

In the Gita, the Knower is one who truly sees how all action is at bottom non-action, suffering.[24] Such a person will not suffer the delusion that life's meaning lies in acting to satisfy our desires and imposing our personal purpose on the world. On the contrary, the

Knower will act with a concentrated mind (*samadhi*). Unconfused by "I-consciousness" and its many objects, such a mind is concentrated on the playing out of the world order, in disciplined action.[25] The Knower is a participant in the great Sacrificial Act that is the world order.

The Confucian Perspective:
The Self

Though the concept of the self in the *Analects* is my focus, the intended larger context is that of Asian thought in some of its major variants, and ultimately the lesson to be learned by the West.

In the various strains of Asian thought, it is a common teaching that the individual self or ego is the source and the seat of delusion, suffering, and spiritual bondage. Our great task, therefore, is to let go of the self. The specific doctrines, differing as they do, nevertheless are significantly akin in their use of bywords with predominantly negative or passive connotation. Examples are "emptiness,"[1] "*neti-neti*,"[2] "non-ego,"[3] "nonaction."[4] The literature of Buddhist orthodoxy in India, of Chinese Taoism, and in effect of Hinduism is replete with such attitudes regarding the individual self.

What seems to be the great exception is the thought whose source is Confucius. Confucius seems to be a yea-sayer. His language and his imagery are generally positive, affirmative, active. A central concern is that each of us dedicate ourselves with utmost vigor and unqualified commitment to making something of ourselves personally. We must vastly develop our learning and our skills,[5] cultivate proper demeanor,[6] develop appropriate attitudes and motives,[7] and strive to act always on right principles.[8] Effort, commitment, determination, persistence, diligence[9]—these are key

This is a substantially revised version of "The Problem of the Self in the *Analects*," *Philosophy East and West* 29, no. 2 (1979): 129–140.

necessities if one is to become what Confucius taught was a truly noble person, a *chun tzu*.

It is my thesis that, nevertheless, Confucius belongs in the more general Asian tradition. So here we have a puzzle.

The path to resolving the puzzle lies in recognizing that the Confucian ideal, the *chun tzu*, is throughout unselfish. The task posed here is to show how these two aspects of Confucius's teaching are really one.

It is the commentators, rather than Confucius, who are tempted to generalize these teachings by focusing on the "self" as an overarching or basic rubric. They sum it all up in terms of "self-cultivation," a term that appears only as a formula in one passage of the *Analects*,[10] probably a later insertion, and is also important in teachings of the post-Confucius generations.[11] Would Confucius himself have generalized on his own teachings, or summarized them by taking the consummately cultivated self as his focal concept? The fact is, of course, that he did not. Why not? He did not do so because he did not mean it.

Yet one cannot read the *Analects* without having the impression that for Confucius there is surely something focally important, in a positive way, about the role of the individual in bringing himself to be as he should be. Thereafter, as Confucius sees it, living as such, the *chun tzu* is a man of true humanity, a truly noble man (*jen*). Is this not self-cultivation?

There have been many discussions of these interrelations—comparisons of Confucians with each other, and with teachers in such other schools as Taoism and Buddhism. I propose here a more independent approach to identifying the respects in which Confucius is radically affirmative as to the self. He advocates cultivating the self, yet teaches a radical selflessness.

In the course of the *Analects* there emerges a concept of the self as a self-observing and self-regulating individual, a self sharply distinct from others. It is a self with interests that may in fact conflict with those of others but that ought ideally to be brought into accord with the interests of others. From this self there arises a kind of directed dynamism—wanting, willing—that characteristically is what mediates between the orientation of the self and the actual conduct of the self. This intermediary dynamic varies in intensity, persistence, direction, and occasion. All these variations are contingent. But what is necessary is that, in each instance, this dynamic is generated and controlled by the self. The locus of this will is the particular self, as distinct from all other selves.[12]

In this summary characterization of the self as having will, there is nothing new or startling to the Western mind, but there is something important to our inquiry. What is important is that on the basis of this portrait we can see quite specific respects in which Confucius is affirmative, rather than negative, about the role of personal will and of the self it expresses. Specifically, Confucius appeals to us to activate our will—something only we as individuals can do—as a prime means of realizing the ideal life. He repeatedly emphasizes that we should commit ourselves unflaggingly to learning and then following the Way (*tao*),[13] and specifically to learning and abiding by the proper forms of social intercourse (the *li*),[14] clinging to humaneness (*jen*),[15] and following the principles of fidelity and reciprocity.[16] All this adds up to the will to become and then the will to remain a *chun tzu*. Professor Creel, the distinguished Confucian scholar, has said, "Confucius demanded the utmost zeal of his followers."[17]

When it comes to control over activating the will, regulating its intensity and persistence and selecting its direction, everything depends upon the use of powers uniquely and distinctively controlled by the self. In achieving the ideal life, it is the self whose zealousness of will must be relied upon, and that unceasingly plays a crucial role. Confucius, as I mentioned at the outset, is the great yea-sayer when it comes to the self as actor, as an individual self acting through its own will. His conception of human nature, real and ideal, is rooted in such affirmation.

The point can be made with more specificity. Reading Confucius's remarks, we find either implicit or expressed the view that the locus of the will is the individual self, which is its generative source, and which has control over its arousal, intensity, and direction and thus in the end its power over conduct. All this is implicit in saying that Confucius is "affirmative" in his attitude to the self.

Yet in the end, we are ideally to be selfless. How can this be?

We need now to identify the negative aspects, the respects in which Confucius teaches, as central to his Way, that we must have no self and not impose our personal will.

We can begin to understand this by recalling Confucius's emphatic rejection of certain kinds of motives and goals. He tells us that we ought to abjure the quest for personal profit,[18] personal fame,[19] or personal gratification of the senses.[20] It is not that there is anything intrinsically wrong with fame, wealth, honor, or even sensual pleasure—such things arise as incidental effects of a will directed to the Way (*tao*) for its own sake. But better to have poor food and shabby clothes and be unknown, and to will the *tao*, than to depart from the *tao* even for a moment.[21] It is the role of the Way, the *tao*, that we have not yet explored.

It will be recalled that my will, in respect to its generative source, control over its arousal, intensity, and direction, and its power in turn over conduct, is inherently personal. For in all these respects my will can only be identified and described by identifying me personally.

Nevertheless, the ground for willing a certain act is distinguishable from any of these, and it need not be personal. It is true that I and only I can will my will, but it may be that what I will is what is called for by the communal norms of action, the *li*, or by loyalty, *chung*, or by the norms of mutuality, *shu*, or the right, *yi*. Or, to put it most generally, what Confucius is teaching is that the ground of our will should be the Way, the *tao*. In other words, my reason for willing as I do should simply and solely be that this is what the *tao* calls for.

Thus it is in this respect that when the ground of my will is the *tao*, my will is not personal. For neither *tao* nor its subsidiary aspects are defined by reference to me uniquely. The *tao* says that any person in my present position should do thus and so—my proper name is not built into the *tao*.

In all aspects of the *tao* there is an inherent generality, an absence of essential reference to a unique individual. My personal existence is contingent; not so the *tao*. The *tao* is not only intelligible independently of such reference, its moral authority is independent of reference to me as the unique entity that I am. Hence, it is true that the will that I direct to the *tao* is personal with regard to its initial locus of energy and its control over the arousal, intensity, direction, and persistence of my action. Yet when it comes to the ground on which I choose and justify the direction for my will, and on which I elect to maintain that will vigorously and wholeheartedly, that ground—the *tao*—is in no way one that has reference to me personally.

Egoists are those who have their will grounded in themselves, in their uniquely personal desires and motivating inclinations. The egoist wants to be famous or wealthy—and here the wealth or fame must be his alone, or it is not an adequate ground of will for the egoist. To look at the ground of an egoist's will is thus necessarily to look at that ego; whereas to look at the ground of a *chun tzu*'s will is to look not at the person but at the *tao*. If one seeks to understand deeply the content of an egoistic will, one must necessarily understand that particular person, the motives, anxieties, hopes, and other personal data that go to make intelligible the conduct of that person.

On the other hand, the more deeply one explores the *chun tzu*'s will, the more the personal dimensions are revealed as purely formal. True, the individual is the unique space-time bodily locus of that will. Yet to understand the content and significance of the *chun tzu*'s will is to understand the *tao*, not the *chun tzu* as a particular person. The ego is the key to the egoist's will. The *tao* is the key to the *chun tzu*'s will.

The egoist's will imposes the egoist on the world. The *chun tzu*'s will imposes nothing, but it manifests or actualizes the *tao*. I say the *chun tzu*'s will does not impose itself, because I mean to emphasize that the *te*,[22] the peculiar power of the *tao*, is not itself will power, although it acts through the will.

Ideally all *chun tzu* participate of their own will, but they do so in spontaneously harmonious ways because it is the *tao* that guides their will. Thus, the egoist, when of higher rank, orders or commands me how to act. Not so the *chun tzu*. The *chun tzu* accomplishes by "yielding"—he yields his will to the *tao*, and never imposes by means of will on others. Thus he leads in virtue of his status as a role model. As Confucius tells us, the *chun tzu* gives no orders.[23]

This total exclusion of the imposition of personal will generates the atmosphere that pervades and distinguishes the *Analects*. The atmosphere is that of an ideal community in which there are no coercive forces but only the spontaneous harmony of the *tao*.

Since the *chun tzu*'s will is thus ideally the medium by which, and through which, the *tao* is allowed and enabled to work and to be actualized, the personal self of the *chun tzu* has become, ideally, transparent.

This conception is in the spirit of Lao Tzu's Taoist teaching, even though Confucius and Lao Tzu are commonly taken to have contrasting views. For example, Lao Tzu says that the sage has no heart of his own,[24] that he does not put himself forward,[25] that he does not seek to dominate,[26] that people do not know him,[27] that he is dark,[28] and simply rides the *tao*.[29]

One gets still another perspective on this view of the *chun tzu* by recollecting teachings in the Bhagavad Gita, teachings to the effect that I am not the actor,[30] that Krishna or Brahman is the true ground of all.[31] In the Gita, one of Krishna's central teachings is that we should not act for the sake of the fruits of the action. It is the *dharma*, not the personal ego, that should govern.[32] The *chun tzu*'s will, grounded in the *tao*, is a will that in an important way is unconcerned for the fruits of action, concerned only for the *tao*.

The idea at issue here is more culturally catholic yet. It is a way of expressing, less pregnantly but in one respect more precisely, the spirit of the phrase, "Not my will, but Thine be done."

I must now qualify my formulation of Confucius's view. His view is more complex and sensitive to human reality than I have indicated up to this point. There is, after all, an important way in which the unique personality can and must have its play. One sees this in the *Analects* in various contexts.

Consider a fine violinist's presentation of the Bach Chaconne, or consider *Chih*, the Chief Musician, and his performance of the "Ospreys."[33] Plainly what governs in a genuinely artistic performance is the musical conception brought forth by Bach, or the poetic-musical conception of the "Ospreys." This musical concept, corresponding by analogy to the *tao*, transcends the individual artist's will, and constitutes the ground of the will for each ideal performance. The essential conception is encoded in the musical score, or in the ancient Chinese Book of Songs; but the musical concept itself is actualized in the developing structure of sound, or word-in-sound, of the actual performance. The performer's will and skills are the medium through which the musical concept becomes actualized.

Yet we know that there are legitimate personal aspects of the musical performance, aspects that are irreducible and valuable. Without the wholehearted and unwaveringly diligent will to follow through properly, there is no performance, or it simply breaks down. Beyond this, the personal dimensions of style, temperament, and interpretation shine in and through the embodied Chaconne. *Chih*'s performance is singled out by Confucius for its special brilliance. Yet, although style and interpretation may be unique to the performer—that is, personal—it remains basic that the true artist's style serves the work. The personal interpretation is a genuine interpretation of the work, not an imposition of qualities external to it. Style and interpretation must reveal, and not dominate, obscure, or distort the concept of the Chaconne or the "Ospreys." Confucius remarks that though the musicians in ancient times were given a certain liberty, the tone remained harmonious, brilliant, consistent, right to the end.[34]

Unique personality has a role because, no more than any concept, even that of the *tao*, the musical concept cannot resolve unambiguously every aspect of the concrete reality to be actualized. No concept embraces the fullness of the reality. And so the performer, the one who makes the music actual, cannot be denied the office of creating a reality that is denser and richer than any concept, and that therefore is necessarily personal in important ways. Yet the personal only serves and enhances the governing and pervading concept, which is nonpersonal.

It would be enlightening to explore further the ways in which this conception of Confucius's significantly differs from conceptions of selflessness peculiar to other streams of Asian thought. Obviously there are differences of importance. Yet if we keep in view his teaching as centered on the *tao* as ground of the will, and on the implications of this grounding, we see clearly a fundamental respect in which he shares in the pan-Asian ideal of selflessness as crucial to salvation.

Responsibility and
Indeterminism

Moral theory has long been plagued by a dilemma. If all that happens in this world is completely causally determined, then it seems to follow that there is no genuine freedom of choice. What I "choose" to do would have been a settled matter eons before my birth. And if so, what sense would it make to hold me morally responsible for my "choices" and actions?

On the other hand, if one supposes that there is a certain amount of causal indeterminism in the world, and if this is true about our choices, then again it seems to follow that I cannot be held responsible for my choices. For indeteminism in regard to choices would imply that no matter what my character, values, or personality, there remains an element of pure chance, a random character to my choice.[1] Then why should I be considered responsible for it? What could it mean to say I am a morally responsible person?

It does not seem to help matters to suppose that my choice is what it is because of my character and personality, or anything of the kind. For in so postulating, one postulates that the choice is determined by these factors, and thus is not free. In any case, if the indeterminism applies to them, then these come to be what they are at least in part free of prior causation, in which case chance enters the picture. And why should one be responsible for acts that flow from a character which has emerged by chance?

Thus, in sum, insofar as there is complete deteminism, it seems there is no freedom and hence no responsibility. But insofar as what we do is not determined by prior causes, then it is insofar a matter of pure chance and hence not something that I should be held personally responsible for. Since the two assumptions—the assumption that complete determinism is true, and the supposition that it is not—allow for no further alternatives, it seems that freedom of choice and personal moral responsibility for one's choices can have no place in our world.

This seeming logical certainty flies in the face of assumptions that are fundamental to the meaning of human life and to our actual beliefs in practice.

The End of Determinism

The theory that every event has the character that it does as the necessary effect of prior causes is, in the end, a theory about facts. As such, it is open to refutation by showing facts to the contrary.

It may seem unimaginable that there could be such contrary facts, but that it is unimaginable merely shows that what we have in mind is a matter of imagination, not necessarily facts. Much that we now know as a result of the research in physics ands biology was unimaginable previously. Moreover much of it cannot even be *imagined* now; we merely assent verbally, accept the authority of the scientists who in turn think in terms of mathematics, laboratory devices, and theories that indirectly reveal the underlying reality. Especially when it comes to microbiology, quantum physics, and cosmic theory, we have to rely on imagery that is primitive, only analogically and in very limited ways akin to the unimaginable but actual reality.

More specifically, the discoveries of the twentieth century, most especially in quantum physics, have revealed that the submicroscopic ultimate elements and processes of our reality are not well described by any theory of universal determinism. What happens at that level, though still not fully understood, nevertheless is radically different from what had generally been taken as axiomatic features of the interrelations of space, time, and material interactions.[2]

The theory of universal determinism was, after all, a philosophical extrapolation, an act of intellectual and scientific faith rather than a well-demonstrated truth. It served as a heuristic assumption that often approximated the world as we knew it. That act of faith no longer has scientific plausibility.

Hence, so far as concerns the dilemma outlined at the outset of this study, one horn of the dilemma can be dispensed with.

The Other Horn of the Dilemma

Declaring universal determinism unsupportable, and ruling it out as a contender in the quest to understand freedom and responsibility, by no means resolves our difficulties. It is because the remaining possibility, indeterminism, is such a puzzling possibility that in recent times a voluminous literature has appeared in which philosophers have tried to avoid it by seizing the first horn of the dilemma and trying to find a way to reconcile determinism with freedom and responsibility. That effort, at bottom, goes for naught once the assumption of determinism loses plausibility.

Nevertheless, having abandoned the premise of determinism, and as a consequence deterministic theories of free will and responsibility, we are left with the problem that it seems difficult or impossible to reconcile indeterminacy of the will with responsible conduct.[3]

The object of this essay is to dispel the seeming irreconcilability of responsibility and indeterminacy of the will. In short, the assumption that indeterminacy and responsibility are incompatible is false. That assumption loses its force if one takes into account two basic facts. One of them is intimately familiar to us, the other not well appreciated. Moreover, the paradoxical relation between these two facts is peculiarly elusive. Yet in order to see the compatibility of indeterminacy and responsibility, it is necessary not only to identify these two basic facts, but also to see the significance of their interrelation. What follows is an explanation and justification of these claims.

The first of the two basic facts that reveal how responsibility is based on indeterminacy is the obvious fact that we do things. We do things in our mind—we reason, we judge, we intend, we calculate, we decide, we hope, we plan, we analyze. And we do things with our body—we perform actions. This first basic fact can be encapsulated in the statement: I am a doer.

Although more must eventually be said about the fact that I am a doer, we can turn now to the second basic fact, less widely appreciated.

This second basic fact can seem to be incompatible with the first. Indeed it can seem to be the denial that the first "fact" is truly fact at all.

The second basic fact is that we are patients, passive recipients of the occurrences that constitute what we are aware of as our doings.[4] To see this we can turn first to what we do mentally. The fact is that my desires, fears, pleasures, and attitudes emerge in me, and their coming to be is not an action of mine, not what I do, but what I find happening in me. More significantly for present purposes, the same holds true of my thoughts, my judgment, my intentions, decisions, and choices. I *find* myself coming to a decision, thinking this, intending that. I intend this or that; but that I come to have this intention is not an act of mine. It is something that happens in my mind.

It is true that when I am thinking I am engaged in mental activity, I am doing something. However, its now coming to be the case that I am thinking this or that thought is not something I do. It comes to be that I think this thought. I find myself thinking this thought or that.

When I consider the choice between A or B, I find at some point that A appeals to me, more than B. Its coming to appeal to me is not something I do; it is something I find happening. I may then find that the resolution, the intent and decision to move towards A rather than B, have emerged in my mind and as my attitude. That I choose A is my action. That this comes to be my choice is not an action of mine. I do not choose the choice. I just choose.

True, there may be preliminary steps I take, actions I perform with the aim of promoting thoughts on a certain topic, or choices of actions of some kind. Yet such prior actions, whether mental or physical, never settle the matter. At the last moment I may find that my thoughts wander elsewhere, or that I choose to act contrary to what I had planned. Or I may find, in spite of all, that I can't seem to come to a decision. Then at some point it happens: I do make the choice. It comes to be what I do—but not necessarily so because of what I did previously. It could have been otherwise.

It is no novel philosophical insight that essentially the same is true of my bodily doings. Each motion I make is a motion that just occurs, a "basic action."[5] I do not have to do anything, there is no method or means I use in order to raise my arm. My arm rises, and I apprehend this as *my* doing because it moves as I intend. Yet the intention in the action is not the cause. The intention does not suffice to bring into being the movement of the arm. This is evidenced by the fact that my arm may not move as intended. It may not move at all; perhaps it is paralyzed. Or it may begin to move as intended and then suddenly deviate and move in some unintended way. I intend my arm to lift the cup neatly, but my arm suddenly moves abruptly and the cup spills.

Much the same can be said about the intention itself. I do not intend to intend. It just is the case that I find that I do intend. That I intended just comes to be. I know no action I can perform that will directly, that is, through some type of causal necessity, bring into being a certain intention. I may see good reasons for adopting a certain intention. Yet the intention may not emerge. I cannot bring myself to adopt the intention. And that is to say that no matter what I do, the intention just does not come into being as the direct and necessary effect. I only know for sure what my intent will be when I actually find myself already with that intent.

We may ask: Although not infallibly effective, not a sufficient cause, isn't my intention to move my arm one of the causes of the bodily motion? The answer, of course, is that this is true in some ill-understood commonsense idiom of "causation." Yet in this common usage there is an acknowledged element of indeterminacy. We understand that, unlike what we may take to be scientific usage, this "cause" may not be followed by the customary "effect." It is very likely true that whatever kind or degree of physical being the intention ultimately has, this plays a role of substantial significance in the physical causal complexes that may be at work in causing my arm to rise. This does not take us very far, however. For we do not know how intentions are related to the physical realm. What we do know is that intentions are commonly implemented in action, but not always. If we do speak of intentions as causing bodily motion, we speak in terms of probabilities, never of certainties, and the notion of "cause" as used here is obscure.

Just as I capsulized the first basic fact in the phrase, "I am a doer," so I have done the same for the second basic fact of our passivity: "I am a patient." I find that I do things, mentally and physically. On the other hand, I also find that I never know for sure what I will find myself doing until I find myself doing it.

It may be well to anchor these rather abstract reasonings in some concrete illustrations of action and passivity as co-attributes of all I do.

Thus, for example, my pen now moves along the page putting into legible shape the series of thoughts and words that come to me. These thoughts and words occur to me in a reasonably steady sequence. I discover what I am about to write as I write it. Yet, of course, from another point of view, I am the doer, it is I who think these thoughts and write them.

It is my good fortune, which I commonly take for granted, that my ideas and hand motions do not occur in random fashion. (Some day they may, and without any action on my part.) At this stage of my life, however, the context, both physical and mental, generally suffices for it to be the case that I think and write in an orderly fashion. I count on this.

Certainly I know little or nothing about whatever physical causes are at work, nor need I. I think of my past learning and experiences—in a vague commonsense way—as causes of what is happening. Yet, again, those "causes" do not suffice to bring about what is happening. They may exist, and may typically play some role, and yet, in spite of that, suddenly nothing relevant, or something only imperfectly or distantly relevant, may occur to me. Occasionally, and happily, a totally unexpected but constructive thought occurs to me. On the other hand, my pen may unexpectedly and unintentionally stray, or may omit or misplace letters. It is an open-ended process, typically fairly predictable, but not more. It is lived as a matter of probabilities, of more or less confident expectations, depending on the total context, but in any case never a certainty.

I remember something now. I have an appointment with Hal in a few minutes. I can just as well say: A certain memory has occurred to me now; it has popped up in my mind. Thinking about our meeting, I take it for granted that upon greeting Hal his name will come to my mind. It usually does. Yesterday, it didn't, and I was disconcerted.

I find in one situation that anger seizes me, though I know it's not reasonable. I find that a fondness for a certain person has developed in me. I find I can't believe what Bob tells me, though I find myself believing Shirley's story. I deplore the desire that arises in me to lash out at Tom. I know I shouldn't, but nevertheless I find myself hoping he will pay dearly for what he did.

Of course, none of these things arise in a vacuum. My background, my character, the circumstances in which I find myself—all of these seem quite obviously to play a role. I see these as major influences ("causes") of what I think, feel, perceive, value, and do. Broadly speaking, most of the things I am doing, both mentally and physically, make sense in the circumstances. That's the way the world is made up, though I'm far from understanding how and why.

Yet for me in regard to what I do, the future always has an element of indeterminacy. The unexpected is always hovering. I live my life accepting that things generally but not necessarily follow certain familiar patterns. I can only describe in a rough and ready way what these patterns are. This rough and ready intuition of how things usually go suffices. This reality is built into my everyday living. It is reality as I am aware of it, as I experience it. It is what reality is for the subject, in that sense subjective.

It is this passive aspect of my experience that accounts for the inescapable perception of my will as what might be called an ur-cause, an original, uncaused cause.[6] In everything I do there is an element of the irreducibly aboriginal in its initiation. It is this that I experience as my "free will," the will that is free to go either way, not the inevitable outcome of what preceded.

Yet this is also the perspective of myself as passive. For what I do has the character of having been indeterminate *until* the doing occurs, and being rendered determinate by that doing. It is, paradoxically, indeterminacy and passivity in regard to what I do that establish what I do as action *ab initio*. Herein lies the justified apprehension of the will as first cause. It is the initiation of meaningful conduct that in some crucial respect(s) has no existential necessity other than the fact that I do it.

Nevertheless, the tendency, especially in the Western traditions, is to focus attention on the active dimension, on the fact that it is I who am willing and doing this. The aspect of passivity goes unnoticed except when some unusual situation arises such as undesirable thoughts that "force" themselves upon us, names, facts, or words that refuse to come forth, actions we suddenly perform that surprise us, perhaps even shock us.

In spite of the passive aspect of our doings, it bears notice that simple observation of everyday life reveals that my deeds are not random events. That is, I do deliberate, and, of course, my character, my hopes and values are in various ways commonly, though not always, reflected in my choices, as is my understanding of the external circumstances. In short, I do commonly act rationally.

How does it come about that this is so? We know a little but not much. We have a variety of elaborate theories about human psychology and biology. Yet rarely can one strictly deduce from the theory the course of everyday human action with any close approximation to the high probabilities afforded by common sense.

The fact is that, generally speaking, we do not need to know these theories in order to get along in life. It is a fact that these sorts of patterns do generally obtain. Our actions typically do substantially reflect who we are and in what circumstances we find ourselves. This is the fact—our ability to explain how, ultimately, it comes about this way is very limited indeed. Nevertheless, it is self-evidently not pure chance, not random.

In dealing with life, and more specifically with questions of responsibility, I take for granted the patterns, their vagueness and variability, as well as their regularity, and their often unpredictable failures to obtain. There are no clear certainties here, but there are often high degrees of probability, as well as degrees or kinds of indeterminacy. This is built into our ways of life, regardless of time or culture.

Against this background we can again raise the question: Why is it reasonable, why is it fair, that I should be held responsible for my acts? Insofar as the choices are indeterminate until done, why is it fair to hold me responsible for my choices? What if my acts turn out to be "not in character" or even, on some occasion, quite inconsistent with my character and values? Why blame me?

The answer lies in our history, in particular the history of how we achieve status as moral agents.

To accept moral status and to achieve social acknowledgement of that status is in effect to enter into a compact. The compact envisions that it is recognized by me and by others that I and my acts are to be clothed in the moral authority that belongs to moral status. This not only provides me with the benefits of moral respect from others. It also means that we reciprocally accept responsibility for what we do, and that we acknowledge that others are entitled to hold us responsible for what we do. This form of life is the foundation of civil community, as contrasted with groups in which human beings would be treated like animals, and power alone would reign supreme.

Encompassed in the compact is the clear recognition that we did not choose our original personal endowments. We evolve from the biological and social circumstances in which we happened to be born, and from the ensuing life experience in our early, preresponsible years. It is self-evident that our adult character and capacities reflect to a substantial degree the circumstances that obtained prior to our arriving at moral status.

This is not inconsistent with viewing the resulting adult as responsible; on the contrary it is the recognized background against which the life of responsibility exists. Community requires that one acknowledge one's identity as one finds oneself, and that one commit oneself to the moral pact that enables the moral community. Life has dealt us our hand; to become responsible, one must begin by playing the hand one has been dealt. We must play the hand. To fail to do so, at least tacitly, is the sign of alienation from one's human community, that is, what we see as mental pathology.

Certainly there are types of situations that justify attenuation of the compact—excuses for what we have done. But whatever the nature of the excuses, they are the exceptional conditions. We need not go into them here because it suffices for the present argument that what has been argued about indeterminism and responsibility holds true for our conduct generally. It is this notion that responsibility is compatible with indeterminism that has commonly been denied.

I cannot know for sure what I will do. But I do initiate, in a radical way, the direction things will take. My choices and my acts make a difference. I do not pick and choose the acts for which I will acknowledge responsibility, and those for which I won't. I take responsibility for what I do (and I expect you to do the same).

So, in sum, we see that, given the element of indeterminacy, the classical assumption of the will as the *ab initio* source of the act is supported. Likewise we can take note of the evident fact that usually there is a high probability that one will choose one of the rational alternatives. On this basis we accept a kind of moral version of strict liability for the occasional acts that surprise us or that are inconsistent with our established character.

It bears note that what has been argued here about the aspect of passivity in what we do has relevance to the dilemma posed in the Bhagavad Gita. The "inaction in action" taught by the Gita does not raise the issue of causation, but it does claim that we are, so to speak, the passive recipients and medium of the thinking, feeling, and doing that we commonly take ourselves to be initiating. Nevertheless, in our thinking, feeling, and doing we are creating our karma, which is truly the fate we must take up. This conception, paradoxical on its face, is another way of addressing the issues I have addressed here in the language of causation rather than spiritual introspection.

Yet in everything that has been said so far about indeterminacy and the passive aspect of our experience, the argument has been in terms of our subjectivity. That is, the passive aspect of my experience is an aspect of how I experience things. The indeterminacy in action is an indeterminacy for me as I contemplate my future action.

This same perspective on action can be extended to include observers. That is, others cannot predict with certainty what choices I will make, even though they often will be able to do so with high probability. But of course high probability implies a probability, though low, of the contrary.

All such observations reflect the content of the subject's or observer's knowledge and awareness. In this sense they are subjective. But what is the "objective" reality? Is there genuine indeterminacy in the world?

The question implies, plausibly, that there is more to the story than any subject is directly aware of. More particularly, it here invites the traditional question: What if all the indeterminacy that we experience as subjects were merely subjective; the fruit of our ignorance rather than the underlying reality? To ask this is to return to the classical question—What if the postulate of universal causal determinism were true? The question may seem the natural one to ask at this point, but I suggest that it seems so mainly by reason of philosophical tradition rather than by the logic of the argument. In fact we can more profitably ask the contrary question now.

What if the world in fact really does embody an element of indeterminacy?

Of course the question is not about the possibility of everything happening with total indeterminacy—a proposition that would be patently false or merely totally incoherent. What we have to ask here is, What if there is an element, or degree, or kind of indeterminacy in all that happens? Would this condition be incompatible with a capacity for rational and responsible action?

It is to this question that we have here developed an answer. An element of indeterminacy is indeed compatible with free and responsible action. Of course the more fully stated truth, as indicated previously, is that the indeterminate nature of the act until performed, rooted in our passive role in its coming to be, is the condition of our personal responsibility for the act's having the determinate nature that it has. After all, it is I who do my acts.

The preceding must be qualified by a limiting condition. Given a particular personality, and a context of significance to that person, the probabilities must be high that any action by the person will embody the election of one of the reasonable alternatives for that person under those circumstances. I will refer to this as the condition of probable rationality. Only on this condition can the moral compact make sense.

Fortunately, and very obviously, the condition of probable rationality holds true. Why it does so raises profound questions that science and philosophy may explore but cannot (yet) fully answer. Nevertheless, it is a fundamental requirement and expectation so long as human life as we know it continues. And it is a brute fact.

Given that indeterminacy is compatible with a life of responsible action, we can still ask, as philosophers in various cultures have asked: What if the world we subjectively experience is not a part of the whole but instead is, in some total and fundamental way, an illusion? There are various theories of the kind—for example, Buddhist, Hindu, and some forms of Christian doctrine.[7] Relevant, too, are theories, such as the still forceful Wittgensteinian view of language,[8] that portrays the very question as confused. Any exploration of such theories would take one into territory far too uncharted to be addressed here.

What we can conclude, however, is that so far as Western secular philosophies go, indeterminacy is an integral feature of personal moral responsibility.

Suffering

I believe that suffering is the one and only way to achieve anything of spiritual value.[1] I do not mean that suffering teaches us a lesson. To suffer is itself the spiritual value, the only one.

The principal obstacle to understanding suffering is that there seems an ineradicable association between suffering and distress. Nevertheless, in the root meaning of suffering this common conception is wrong.

The first step toward enlightenment here is to see that "to suffer" is a deeply ambiguous verb. The older, more fundamental and still viable meaning of "suffer" does not necessarily convey the idea of pain or distress. Although our inquiry is not merely a linguistic one, it is nevertheless important to clarify our definition of this key term.

The *Oxford English Dictionary* gives some twenty separate meanings of the English word "suffer." The linguistic roots of the word are Latin. The first root is *sub*, meaning "under." The second root is *ferre*, meaning "to bear." Cognate versions of the word, with the same Latin roots, exist in Spanish, French, and Italian.[2]

As the first principal set of meanings in English, the O.E.D. gives "to undergo, to endure." The second principal set of meanings is "to tolerate, to allow." Many of the other meanings in the first set, but not all of them, imply that what is undergone is painful. However this

This is a revised and translated version of "Sufrimiento," in *Religion y Sufrimiento*, ed. Cabrero and E. Nathan, 11–21 (Mexico City: Universidad Nacional Autónoma, 1996).

is not true for the definitions in the second set. The various meanings in the latter set are primarily explained in terms of allowing or permitting something or someone to be or to act without interference. This latter set reflects older usages that have become literary or even archaic or obsolete. Essentially the same points are made in the *Unabridged Webster's International Dictionary*, Second Edition. The same usage exists in Spanish, French, and Italian. All these languages use cognates of "suffer" to mean "allow."

When "suffer" is used to mean "to tolerate," "to allow," "to permit," "not to interfere," we find it in a classic instance of English use. The King James version of the New Testament has Jesus saying, "Suffer the little children to come unto me. . . ." [3] Here "suffer" clearly means "do not interfere," "do not forbid," "let it be," and suggests, if anything, the contrary of pain or distress.

A closely related term with cognates in all these languages[4] is "patient." It is no mere coincidence that we read of "the patience of Job." This will puzzle anyone who examines the Old Testament text of Job and who takes "patience" to be used in the predominantly modern usage. Today "patient" generally implies one who bears quietly, not raising a fuss. But Job was not mild, not deferential, and not quiet. On the contrary, he rants and roars, page after page, unceasingly challenging (blasphemously) the Lord himself with being unjust. Job was patient, however, in the sense that he suffered, he endured, he bore the pain and the grief rather than lying or engaging in self-deception. He was a man who no matter what the cost refused to avoid pain by confessing hypocritically to sins he never committed and begging forgiveness for them. His willingness to bear the pain rather than to lie and break faith with God opened the way for the Divine revelation of Reality to him.

"Patience" has as its root "passive." In modern colloquial usage, the "patient" in the doctor's office may in fact be impatient—agitated and unwilling to wait. Nevertheless the term "patient" is used here in its primary sense. The patient is "the one who is acted upon," the one who is passive and endures without interfering, the one who suffers the physician to act. This suffering need not entail pain; indeed it may entail relief and comfort.

What I have been saying may seem to be merely about words. It is indeed about words, but it is also about human existence. It is true that the linguistic cognates of "suffer" that I have mentioned up to this point all belong to much the same family of languages. So it may seem that I am taking advantage of an accident of linguistic history. But many centuries have passed since these languages—and their respective societies—have gone their different ways. Yet the underlying concept has remained stable through time. That is because there is at work here not just a word but a fundamental human concept.

It is notable that within European civilization, but in a non-Latinate language family, and in connection with an entirely different linguistic root, we see the same concept. The word is the German "leiden." This, too, carries the meaning of suffering pain. Yet here, too, there is the more general concept of simply allowing or tolerating and not interfering.

Still more fundamental proof of the ubiquity of this ambiguous concept emerges when we turn to entirely different civilizations. The same fundamental meaning of suffering and its central spiritual role play a key role in Asian civilizations. Unfortunately, translations of texts from other cultures into Western languages have generally missed this point.

In effect, suffering is the central theme of one ancient, enormously influential Chinese work, Lao Tzu's *Tao Te Ching*. This text speaks of a wondrous power, the *de*, that arises from following the Way. In turn, the Way is repeatedly characterized as the way of *wu-wei*, of no-action, letting things be, letting things happen, going *with* them instead of acting *on* them. The core of Lao Tzu's teaching is expressed in the paradoxical epigram *wei wu-wei*[5]—act through no-action. In other words, even in acting one is to suffer the Way to have its way. Don't impose your own way. The imagery of passivity dominates the language of Lao Tzu.

Lao Tzu's book of the Way and of its marvelous power is replete with evocative, typically paradoxical admonitions. They teach not only the power but also the fulfillment that comes from authentic suffering. He regularly refers to the one who suffers the Way to go its way as the wise one, the sage. The sage, says Lao Tzu, relies on actionless activity, wordless teaching.[6] The sage stays back, and so is ahead.[7] Lao Tzu asks, Which of you can make yourself inert to become in the end full of life?[8] Banish wisdom, discard cleverness . . . diminish the self and curb the desires.[9] To become straight, let yourself be bent; to become full, be hollow. The sage does not strive, therefore no one can contend with him.[10] I know, says the sage, the value of action that is actionless.[11]

The problem of translating classical Chinese terms into European languages can easily obscure the relationships among the ideas. It is notable that the word "suffering" or its cognates do not appear in translations of Lao Tzu. The modern translators do not use this concept because they are dominated by the sense of the word "suffering" that implies pain. Nevertheless, in spite of the word's absence in the translations, once one fixes clearly in mind the generic meaning of "suffering," it becomes clear that the concept is central to the *Tao Te Ching*. Suffer the Way to be. Do not interfere. Be like water—passive, and yet in the end powerful.

In a much later Chinese perspective—that of Chan [Zen] Buddhism—the same basic theme emerges. The great Sixth Patriarch, Hui Neng, in his seminal teachings known as *The Platform Scripture*, characterized the supreme enlightenment as utter openness, utter abandonment of the imposition of ego. He composed the following verses:

> Perversity at work—affliction;
> Correctness at work—no affliction;
> Neither perversity nor correctness at work—Purity;
> Perverse views lead into the world.
> Correct views lead beyond the world.
> Throw both away—Wisdom emerges.[12]

In the great civilization of ancient India, the Bhagavad Gita centers once again on the same basic theme.

The doctrine of *karman* (action) embodies as a central paradox the idea of the "action in inaction," and "the inaction in action" (*karmani akarma/akarmani ca karma*). The Gita says that he who understands this karmic concept is wise.[13] Such a person has "abandoned attachment to the fruits of action"[14]—so that, even when engaging in action, one "does nothing."[15] Constant in success or non-success, even when he is acting [the yogin] is not bound.[16]

Once again we see that, amidst all the complexities of the Gita's teachings, a central theme is the "discipline" (*yoga*) of complete openness, of openness to what is, openness to what "has to be done."[17] This implies one is not dominated by the questions: What do I want? What do I get out of this?

This inaction-in-action is the passivity that liberates spiritually. It does not necessarily bring pleasure or joy, though it may well do so. It is a form of fundamental indifference to pleasure and pain.[18] It is what in the words of European languages can be described as authentic suffering.

It may be well to note that, once again, problems of translation obscure the identity (and universality) of the concept that lies behind the differing words and linguistic traditions. The Sanskrit word often translated into European languages as "suffering" is the word *duhkha*. Indeed it is in the context of "defining" *duhkha* to imply pain that the Sanskrit scholar, Professor Eliot Deutsch, poses the question why suffering should have spiritual value.[19]

I believe that in the Gita the notion of *duhkha* is not well translated as "suffering." The term is appropriately translated into English as "pain," or "misery," or "sorrow," or in any case as a generalized form of distress or malaise. However, what is distinctive about the yogin is not that he is freed from *duhkha*, but that he is freed from the attachment to pleasure and to avoidance of pain. For the yogin, pain and pleasure are "the same."[20] The Gita says, "this disconnection from union with *duhkha*,"[21] is not an absence of pain but a spiritual condition in which, "by no [*duhkha*] however heavy, is he moved."[22] This implies that the yogin can experience intense *duhkha* but is not moved by it. To say that pleasure and *duhkha* are "alike" to the yogin does not mean, of course, that he cannot distinguish between them. It means he suffers both with equal openness, equal readiness to bear them for what they are. He does not try to make the world go his way.[23]

Analysis of *duhkha* reveals that even the notion of suffering pain is itself ambiguous. Built into our usage is often the assumption that pain and distress are our enemies. But there is a dramatic and objectively verifiable difference between suffering pain as a fact, and making pain into an enemy.

It is a well-established medical fact that the physical pain people experience is commonly 30 to 40 percent anxiety-generated—the "enemy" aspect—rather than physically caused by the initial ailment.[24] That is why the placebo effect is so powerful in ameliorating pain. The expectation of relief results in a marked diminution of experienced pain. In short, one's attitude to pain makes a major difference in the experience of pain.[25]

The concept of suffering plays a major role in certain Western philosophical-religious lines of thought as well as Eastern ones. Patience is not only central in the Book of Job, it is also the core of the New Testament teaching of humility and *caritas.* Jesus taught acceptance of all creatures, sinners as well as the pious. Christian humility is deeper than, and different from, meekness. Jesus was not meek.

In the Western mystical tradition we see the same concept in such a teacher as Meister Eckhart. Eckhart compared the enlightened one's disinterested engagement in the world of joys and sorrows as a condition akin to that of a swinging door. The door swings back and forth, while all the time the hinge at the center remains fixed and solid. God, said Eckhart, "is love"; but he also said that God is "immovably disinterested." To understand how these two assertions express a single coherent thesis is to understand authentic suffering.[26]

The question remains, however: Why should it be that "suffering"—letting be, being open—takes on in modern times the implication of distress, unhappiness, pain? ("Passivity" has come to have negative connotations, too, and for analogous reasons, as will be seen.) Why has the aspect of joy been lost from sight in the experience of suffering? Indeed, why does joy in suffering seem a contradiction in terms or a masochistic perversion?

In the modern West, self-assertion is a fundamental value. To be patient is to be frustrated, whereas to act and to shape the course of events to one's liking is to be gratified. The concept of responsibility takes on importance in Western thought because it is the idea that when we impose our will, there should be limits. We assert ourselves, but we should do so responsibly.

It follows that where this attitude of self-assertion predominates, to suffer is to be defeated. Passivity signifies debility, which in turn brings pain, distress, humiliation. Is it any wonder that in such a culture the notion of suffering has come to imply distress?

Although there is much truth in saying that ours is an age of self-assertion, it is also true that in many ways we are characteristically patient. We do suffer authentically. Some of the clearest examples of this can be seen in the area of the arts.

Listening to music can be adulterated by the assertion of one's own ego, one's personal thoughts, feelings, wishes. As a young man I used to listen to Tschaikovsky's *Romeo and Juliet* overture, and part of my intense reaction was due to the projection into the music of my own romantic thoughts and sentiments. I made the music serve my purposes.

On the other hand, whether listening or performing, there now are quite often stretches of time where there is only the music present to me. *I* am totally absent. I let the music live its life. I listen or play in a way such that the music governs. What is happening in the music is all that is happening so far as my consciousness goes.

This is inaction-in-action, *wu-wei*. On such occasions it is the demands of the music that elicit and control my finger and bow action. I simply do, as the Gita says, what "has-to-be-done." If my ego does assert itself, I am likely to falter. The music must be in total control if the music is to be played successfully. In short, I let myself be the medium, not the master. I must patiently suffer the music to live through me. When this happens perfectly, the music lives.

Such suffering is by no means restricted to the context of the arts. It is to be seen—or, sadly, not seen—in the way we experience our emotions and feelings. We often speak of wisdom as the condition of deep and realistic understanding. We are so often not wise, and this is the evidence of our inability to open ourselves to our feelings or failures.

It often takes suffering in the form of pain to force us to confront our vulnerability and our self-deceptive ego. For this reason we infer that spiritual growth is the fruit of painful suffering. Here lies the source of deep confusion. We associate wisdom and humility with a necessary history of pain.

To be open to one's feelings, or to be open to one's relation to another person, may be a joyful experience. It depends on the character of that which is suffered.

The spiritual value of suffering lies in wonder, in the life of openness to reality and its myriad transformations.

13

Out of the Whirlwind: The Book of Job

The law and its themes, concepts, images, and language permeate the Book of Job.[1] The Book of Job is unique among the Hebrew-Christian canonical texts in the manner of its concern with law. Other texts are dogmatic. They promulgate God's laws or commands. They make assertions about the meaning of God's law for us.[2] The Book of Job, however, is analytical, philosophical. Even in so legalistic a culture as that of ancient Israel, Job is the only canonical work devoted to extended, radically critical exploration of such fundamental concepts as law, justice, and retribution. What is surprising is that in the commentaries on Job we rarely find appreciation that the conception of law is central to the argument of the book.[3]

Yet, provocatively, although the Book of Job is explicitly cast in the concepts, language, and imagery of the law, it is presented in the mode of a dramatic poem culminating in a Divine Whirlwind. The poetic dramatic mode is no mere façade. This work is widely acknowledged as surpassingly great in the history of literature.[4] It is intense, it is grand, it is ruthless in its scorn for falsehood and sham. The medium of the message is itself part of the message: the Book of Job is anti-legalist. The poem teaches, instead, a passionate personal integrity as essential to achieving ultimate wisdom and salvation. Law, in turn, is revealed as an essentially human, not divine, enterprise.

This is a substantially revised version of "The Meaning of Law in the Book of Job," Centennial anniversary issue, *Hastings Law Journal* 29, no. 6 (1978): 1581–1617.

Old Testament religion is one of the great sources of the idea that a primary mode, perhaps *the* primary mode, of our relation to God is that of responsibility to his law. On this view, God's will is our law.[5] Even the authority of human law lies in its claim to express, or at least to implement, God's law.

The idea of the pious man who suffers is found in Babylonian[6] and other Near Eastern[7] religions, and in this regard the story of Job— without the theme of law—was a familiar pattern far beyond Israelite culture. But the life and culture of the Israelites became increasingly permeated by priestly legalism.[8] The Genesis story tells of Adam and Eve, and of Noah and the great flood. Thus we see at the very beginning disobedience against God's will by the first human beings, and the punishment that resulted. The story then continues to the Commandments and to laying out the Lord's many supplementary laws and regulations.

Thus there is a deepening consciousness of the human relation to God as one that is a covenant embodied in his will as law.[9] Keeping the covenant assures God's blessings, whereas failing to do so assures his retribution. This doctrine, though at first defined with reference to the nation, later comes to be interpreted as referring to the individual as well.[10]

The idea of existence as framed by God's law also emerges in the doctrines of great Christian thinkers, both Catholic and Protestant.[11] It still permeates Jewish and Christian folk attitudes today.

A perennially troublesome issue for this view has arisen in connection with the concept of retribution and reward. To many people this doctrine has seemed a self-evident corollary of the belief in God the Lawgiver, and of human law.[12] But even before Job, true believers had raised the piercing query: why, then, do the wicked seem to prosper? And why do the righteous seem to suffer?[13] Unbelievers may be inclined to stand aside, bemused by what seems to them a specious and unnecessary dilemma in the first place. But it turns out that things, even so, are not that simple. Job has things to say to the unbeliever, too.

Certainly Job's three "comforters" insist that our life here on earth is ruled by God's law and his justice. As a consequence they believe that he makes the righteous to prosper and the unrighteous to perish.[14] Job, too, has always believed this. Indeed this belief is what eventually motivates his challenges to God in the course of the dialogues.[15]

The centrality throughout the debate of this belief in inevitable reward or retributive punishment may weaken the philosophical persuasiveness of it for so unorthodox an age as ours. Nevertheless, I believe that it has an aspect of profound and necessary truth. I hope to show that the doctrine of retribution is not archaic or a magical view of existence.[16]

On the other hand, we also need appreciate the inadequacy of Job's belief in reward and punishment as an ultimate perspective. In the end, the Lord addresses Job[17] "Who is this that darkeneth counsel by words without knowledge?"

But here I have been talking of final things, and it is the voyage that gives sense and significance to the end. We must go back to the beginning, because the Book of Job is fraught with paradox. The logic of the entire affair is easily obscured. The text itself is "probably more corrupt than that of any other biblical book."[18] So let us return to the beginning and pursue the case from the first moment when "the satan," the prosecutor,[19] accuses Job before Yahweh's court.

The book begins by setting the ultimate issue for us. That issue must remain unknown to Job and his friends if the prosecutor is to develop the evidence. Therefore the ultimate issue is defined in secret. The issue is defined in a context that is sharply separated from the context of Job's ordeal. The book opens with a prologue.

The prologue,[20] based on folk legend, is cast in a self-consciously folk-tale style. Once upon a time there was a great and prosperous and pious man of Uz, named Job. He is mentioned as a very model by the Lord Yahweh himself to his assembled court in heaven. Yahweh challenges the satan, his prosecutor, and asks him, "Have you considered my servant Job? You will find no one like him on earth, a man of blameless and upright life, who fears God and sets his face against wrongdoing."

The satan challenges the truth of this description of Job. "Has not Job good reason to be God-fearing?" The satan points out how God has protected Job from all dangers, piled up his possessions, and showered him with honor, good fortune, and great family.[21] The evidence that this behavior is motivated by self-interest and not genuine piety is easily obtainable, says the satan: "Only take away all these good things from Job, and I'll stand pledge if Job doesn't end up cursing you, my Lord."[22] "Make him ache and suffer in his very bones and flesh and skin! You'll see, I swear!"[23]

It is thereupon agreed that Job will be tested. It is really Yahweh's entire enterprise that the satan's counterchallenge puts on trial. For it was said,

> What then O Israel, does the Lord your God ask of you?—Only to fear the Lord your God, to conform to all his ways, to love him and to serve him with all your heart and soul. This you will do by keeping the commandments of the Lord and his statutes . . . which I give you this day for your good.[24]

If Job is a fraud, Yahweh's relation to the people has failed. If Job is vindicated, we shall have seen the difference between rational self-interest, and true love and fear of God.

It should be remarked, before going further, that the issue from this heavenly perspective is *not* one that centers on law. It is certified by Yahweh himself that Job is a man blameless and upright in his *conduct*. The question raised by the satan concerns Job's true *motives*. Thus in heaven the issue is sharply defined in terms of the state of the soul rather than, as in law, the conduct of the outer man. We, the audience, are witnesses to the heavenly deliberations, we are allowed to see the great issue at trial.[25] As we shall see, it is Job who defines the issue in terms of law.

Yahweh eventually authorizes the satan to deprive Job of every possible good except his very life and consciousness. Family, possessions, honor, physical health—all may be destroyed by the satan except life and consciousness.

This formerly great chieftain thereupon finds himself, both literally and symbolically, on the garbage heap.

In the folk-tale prologue, Job—"patient Job"—endures and prays: "Naked I came from the womb. Naked I shall return whence I came. The Lord gives and the Lord takes away. Blessed be the name of the Lord."[26]

So we have our answer. Job's faith and devotion to the Lord did not depend on rewards. But this answer, true enough in its way, does not give us the kind of answer we want and need. We now know from his behavior that Job's motives were not self-interested. The matter should end there. Yahweh's point has been proven, the satan defeated.

Yet the real story just begins. Job cries out, Why punish me when I have not sinned against the law?

Now the folk tale ends, and its characters leave the stage. There is a radical shift from one literary mode to another, from pseudo-primitivist folk tale to intensely dramatic and passionate poetry, from swift-moving narrative to patient examination of the issues. From the language of naiveté we move to the language of heart's agony and blasphemy, from myth time to the burning present.

This radical shift serves to induce a kind of repression of the prologue. Job and his friends are utterly absorbed in his ordeal as they understand it. They have no suspicion of the real reason for Job's suffering. If they were aware of the real reason for Job's ordeal, the ordeal would lose its point.

The reader's consciousness is also dominated by Job's understanding of the events. For the reader, too, must live through, vicariously, the movement from total despair and misery to complete and understandable acceptance.

Indeed, it may be just because the poem-drama so fascinates and dominates attention that many commentators have mistakenly taken the central issue to be as defined by Job. Commentators have failed to appreciate the truly central issue, as defined in the prologue, and on which the whole book turns.[27]

Now the poem proper begins. Despair, anger, bitterness, fierce attitudes, awful challenges, and radical, tough-minded thought are the stuff of this ordeal. False piety, meekness, or lip service to religious platitudes will not do for Job.

In the beginning, it is Job's sheer despair that shatters the silence. Job's blasphemous reaction to disaster is to curse the day he was born. The three friends who have come to comfort him will not let him settle for such an attitude. They begin by insisting that Job, so strong in regard to the ordeals of others, must now be strong enough to face his own suffering.[28] They define the issues in terms of God's justice, with its implication that Job has sinned.

If we walk in his way, observe his law, then of course we prosper. If we stray, however, he makes us suffer, and we perish.[29] Therefore, Job's suffering may not be viewed merely as misery; it must be viewed as punishment. Job must have failed to act righteously.[30] They argue that until Job confesses his guilt, accepts his punishment, and repents, he is compounding his lack of good faith before God and his guilt.[31] Job's friends remind him that these are the precepts the wise ancients taught us.[32] They persistently press Job to be honest, confess and repent.[33]

This perspective does indeed arouse Job. It provokes him out of his blind despair. Job ever more emphatically and outspokenly picks up the challenge. But his response to this challenge is not what the friends expected. He does accept the challenge to face the truth. He also accepts the framework of God's justice: the guilty are punished, the pious are rewarded. Nevertheless, Job does not reach the same conclusion as his friends. He knows he has not sinned.

"O if only my miseries would be weighed in the scales of justice!" he cries, they would outweigh anything wrong I could have done.[34] It is incomprehensible, but God is persecuting me.[35] Why was I ever born? Why does He not finish the job and mercifully put me to death?[36] What have I done to deserve this? You, my friends, have betrayed me. You spout words and theories and chop logic.[37] I can recognize truth from falsehood, right from wrong. You have put my integrity in question. This quality you may not take from me; no one can do that.[38] How can you look at my suffering and blithely say I deserved this? You don't face realities; you just talk old platitudes that in this case are lies.[39] Where, oh where, is God's justice?

The friends insist because in their view God does necessarily reward the righteous and punish the wicked. They charge Job with blasphemy for maintaining that the law is on his side as against God! Although lacking evidence, they accuse Job of a variety of specific sins in order to defend their theory.[40]

In spite of this, Job presses his claim of having been a truly pious person. Indeed Job increasingly commits himself to the proposition that he is not alone in his unfair suffering. In this world we see it all around us, he alleges. It is the wicked who prosper, and it is the innocent whom they exploit.[41]

Obviously Job's dilemma arises because he is still assessing the matter in terms of law and the principle of necessary retribution and reward.

Job's premises lead logically in one direction: go to law. Yet he despairs. Job ruminates: Even if a man would try to appeal his fate and argue his case, God will not answer! How could a mere human being summon him to law?[42] How could one force him to answer one's charges? Why does he not state his case against me openly, draw up an indictment? I would proudly respond to the indictment. I would present my defense in full, nothing more nor less than the record of my entire life. He, who knows all, ought to be my witness in my defense.[43] And yet, even if he were to appear, how could I choose the proper arguments and answer his questions, when I am terrified by his awfulness and stand here crushed by his power? [44] If only there could be an arbitrator who could assume authority over us both and hear the case! [45] Or if only I had someone strong and free to serve as my advocate! [46] I have been on the right side of the law all my life, and I charge that the Judge has turned not merely prosecutor but unjust persecutor! [47]

There is courage here, but there is incoherence and blasphemy too. Job's legalistic logic, as he himself sees, leads to its own *reductio ad absurdum*. It is his utter truthfulness before God that leads to blasphemy.

It is essential to be aware that in all this Job is not a presumptuous man before God. "Why do you follow me," he calls to the Lord, "and catch me out in every little thing? I am your creature, made by you and totally in your power to the end. Why should you torment your own creature this way?"[48] Job has no false modesty, but neither does he have false pride.

Job asks, "What is man that thou makest much of him?"[49] The echo of the psalm[50] whose language he borrows serves as background to Job's humility. But Job uses the same idea and turns it into a challenge: How could God take such insignificant creatures as worthy targets of his wrath? Although Job apparently rejects the teaching of the psalm, nonetheless the poet, in so speaking, has Job tacitly frame his ordeal within the perspective of the psalm. The poet has highlighted the issue of human dignity. It is this dignity that radiates from Job in his ordeal, even as he sits on the dung heap, a poor, miserable, intellectually confused, morally disarrayed, physically pustulant old man.

To what extent is Job's dilemma real for us? Once we readers, by an act of suspension of belief, grant to Job and his friends their naïve credulity, the dilemmas it creates can elicit our sympathy. But can we truly have empathy, can we participate even vicariously? Have not even theists in modern times got beyond such primitive notions? Can we take seriously the idea that God's law for us implies inevitable rewards and punishments? And, if not, can even the believer really take the Book of Job seriously?

My own belief is that we are wrong if we are patronizing or condescending to Job and his friends. The doctrine that under law, the disobedient are punished and the law-abiding are rewarded is not merely a tenet of some special theological doctrine. After all, the general concept that obedience to law—legal or moral—can only be motivated by fear of punishment is still widely accepted.

Up to this point I have purposely stated the problem without differentiating such notions as piety, integrity, righteousness, uprightness and obedience. Now, however, I want to press what I consider to be the fundamental issue: the nature of obedience. I propose to restate the Old Testament theme that our central spiritual task results from God's laying upon us the requirement that our will shall be in conformity to his will.[51]

This task is not necessarily a moral task. It has a moral dimension if God's will is conceived of as a good will. The question of reward and punishment has generally been thought to be linked to the moral aspect of the situation, but I think this analysis is in error. In the Old Testament there is no clear evidence that God's will is a moral will. What needs emphasis here is that God rules through his will, that is, the dominion of his will over ours.

We need to recognize the phenomenon of the dominion of one will over another as a distinctive relationship. Even if it is an evil will that dominates another will, the relation of one will dominating another remains constant. Generally our will can be subject not only to a dominant personal will but also to some other suitable force such as law or custom.

I want to bring out how and why punishment and reward are inextricably linked to dominion over human will no matter how it occurs.[52] It follows that the assumption that God is Almighty, far from allowing God to forego punishment and reward to achieve his will, makes the link all the more indissoluble.[53]

Dominion over the will is a phenomenon very familiar to us. Suppose, for instance, that I am your superior officer in the military, your supervisor on the job, or a judge issuing an order to you. Here I am exercising power over your will, not your body. The difference is this: if I grab you and hold you, I am exercising power over your body, but if I give you an order, the immediate object of my power is your will. It is my intent that your will should conform to my order. And it is my expectation that you do have the power to obey. However, giving you an order presupposes that you also have the power to disobey me.

This necessarily holds true of God's laws, too. God may command us to act in certain ways. In doing so he exercises his dominion over our will. But this kind of exercise of dominion, if it is to make any sense, implies that he does not physically compel us. He requires that our will conform to his will. This requirement in turn only makes sense if he leaves us the power to act of our own will, the power to obey or to disobey.

So often the drama of the Old Testament is the drama of the disobedient children of God. This is a drama inherent in any relationship that turns on exercising dominion over the will.

Now we have to go farther. Suppose that you do not comply with my order as your commanding officer. What remains to be done? If I do nothing then my order turns out to have had no force, no power at all over your will. I said, "Do so and so." But you do not do it. Thus I have not constrained your will at the time of the order. Nor have I constrained your will subsequent to your disobedience. In short, I have failed to dominate your will. So the verbal form of what I said may have been that of an order, but apparently it was not seriously meant as such. Or perhaps I changed my mind after giving the order and I decided it should not be enforced. In any case, although I say you must do it, your power to do as you willed has in no way been curbed.

There is only one way out of this dilemma if there is to be a command or law having force. It is the universal, age-old way: I must in some way constrain, curb, or humble your will because of your disobedient act. If there is to be a constraint on your will, it must be imposed subsequent to the act because the order cannot enforce itself.

To constrain, humble, or crush the will is, of course, the very core of what is classically meant by suffering. To suffer is to endure that over which our will has no power, that which is against our will. To suffer is to be the patient, not the agent. "Behold, we count them happy which endure. Ye have heard of the patience of Job. . . ."[54]

How does one humble a person's will and make a person suffer? Among the universally effective forms of humbling the will are the infliction of physical pain, the deprivation of access to home or to loved ones, or the loss of liberty, or honor, or property. These acts are ubiquitous forms of punishment because they are generally contrary to what human beings will.

So the paradox of dominion over the will is that the dominator's hand is forced. There is no meaningful alternative to punishing the disobedient. It is not that punishment necessarily deters future disobedience. It is that the idea of laying down a law, order, or command loses its significance if not conjoined with the policy that the consequence of disobedience will be punishment, humbling of the will.

This paradox intensifies when we assume that God's central relation to us is expressed in terms of his will or law. Then even the Almighty is bound by this necessity intrinsic to law. He has no option. He must punish me for disobedience. It becomes empty verbiage if I say that I am subject to God's law, if I also know that I have the power to disobey without suffering any punitive consequences. If this were so, it would amount to saying that he leaves me free to do as I will.

The paradox of dominion over the will is that the dominator is compelled to impose punishment for disobedience. Thus the subordinate ultimately gains a certain crucial element of control over the dominator. Even if the dominator is God, if I will to disobey, I compel him to punish me.

A human lawgiver must have a policy of punishing disobedience, though any of a number of eventualities may intervene to prevent the punishment. One obvious eventuality in the case of human law is that the offender cannot be found. But for an all powerful God who cannot be turned from his purpose,[55] there are no such eventualities. Once he has decided what his will is, God then has no choice but to punish me if I disobey. And whether or not I disobey is of course up to me.

A final result, more interesting yet, is that if I choose to comply with the Lord's will, he must not punish me. He must, in effect, reward me. This idea needs a brief further explanation. Imagine that a professor says to the student: "You are required to turn in a term paper by next week; if you fail to do so, you get an F. On the other hand, if you do turn it in on time, you also get an F." What possible sense can be made of that statement? It is an absurd way of talking. But if the professor is serious, this must be his odd way of indicating that the term paper is irrelevant. By contrast, if he really means to impose the demand upon the student, it must make a difference whether or not the student obeys. So, too, even if it is the Lord commanding us how to act, our compliance or noncompliance has to make a difference.

It might be thought that if the command is a moral one, then punishment and reward are unnecessary. Yet it is unintelligible to say that God, or anyone, wills that someone should act in a morally right way, and then to assert further that morally wrong action will have no consequences (except for the label). At most, his "will" becomes no more than friendly advice.

I am not, of course, saying that Job and his friends had developed precisely the analysis that I have been presenting. I have given an explicit analysis of what I believe was intuitively perceived by these and other thoughtful and religious individuals in the Judeo-Christian tradition. It is a truth that is readily blinked at by those who at one and the same time hold to belief in God as just lawgiver and judge, and who yet remain skeptical about the inevitable triumph of virtue over vice.

Given this insight, then, Job is inevitably driven to the highest pitch of moral despair and confusion. He feels that, if this is a world of law, then his suffering must signify either his guilt or God's failure justly to enforce the law. What does not yet enter Job's mind is the more radical implication of the fact that in this world the innocent suffer, and the wicked often prosper. On the analysis that I have given, that fact implies that the concept of God-as-lawgiver is incoherent and inapplicable to the reality of our existence.

It is this logically implied truth—the irrelevance of the concept of law in relation to God—whose truth Job will discover in an experiential revelation.

We now can return to the story itself. We left Job in that abyss of despair in which he charges God with injustice, and yet paradoxically claims confidence that his case will be judged justly. His faith in God remains, and so does his loyalty, though his logic is hopelessly against him. He has pressed the issues to the limit; whereas the friends have only succeeded in provoking him into this allegation against God and defense of his own integrity.

It is important to note that by this point Job has given up hope that he can contend directly with the Lord.[56] He cries in desperation, for an arbitrator or intermediary. In any case, he maintains his innocence, and refuses to make false confession before the Lord in order to cease his suffering.[57]

Suddenly, unannounced, there appears on the scene a young man, Elihu. He is bursting with the message he brings. He charges Job with presumptuousness. Elihu proclaims that Job, a mere man, is accusing the Lord of purposely perverting justice! What a thirst for irreverence![58] This is in a way puzzling. Job's agony seems justified. As Job says, "Though I am in the right, I am condemned out of my own mouth for saying so!"[59]

Elihu reasserts familiar views and attitudes, but he puts them in a new perspective. "Look up at the sky and then consider, observe the rain clouds towering above you: How does it touch him if you have sinned? However many your misdeeds, what does it mean to him? If you do right what good do you bring him, or what does he gain from you?"[60]

Then Elihu gives a flat answer: "Your wickedness touches only men, such as you are; the right that you do affects none but mortal man."[61]

Elihu also announces that wisdom comes in suffering.[62] He says we must reach the depths of suffering, hopelessness, and helplessness before God may send a being to intercede or to ransom us for a new life.[63]

This idea, again, is a new twist on an old idea. Job himself had earlier expressed the faith that he would be vindicated by a *goel*, an avenger or ransomer.[64] But now the suffering is portrayed not as mere grievance to be avenged or righted. It is instead the holy medium through which God transmits his teaching. Only when all hope is abandoned can the message be effective and the *goel* at last appear.

This teaching raises a puzzle that we must examine. That we become wise through suffering and that we need an intercessor are familiar ideas. But we need to understand why this is so. There is here an internal necessity, a necessity linked to the concept of the will. To suffer is to be compelled to endure, undergo, and experience the humbled will, rather than to be able to act and impose one's will. The message of suffering is thus implicit in suffering itself. Wisdom is what is revealed to the truly humble will.

This concept of wisdom is basic to teachings other than that of the Old Testament Book of Job. It is at the core of the teachings of the Bhagavad Gita, Buddhism, Lao Tzu, Confucius, and Jesus.[65]

Elihu now puts another idea in a new way. Eliphaz, Job's friend, had earlier alluded to horrible nightmares in which he had presumed to put himself in the right as against God.[66] Job, too, had spoken of nightmares that he viewed as visitations of persecution by the Lord.[67]

Elihu says that God does speak to man in dreams. But he does not do so to persecute. What he teaches is a great lesson about man's false pride in hoping to master life on his own terms.[68] This lesson of the night is not a lesson that demeans, weakens, or darkens. Properly understood, these dreams give strength.

God speaks to us not only in dreams but in songs,[69] says Elihu. Listen to the songs in the night, he says, behold the visions of night. Accept me, says Elihu, as one who will intercede. Surrender your will and instead exalt God and this life that is his creation. Be lifted up not by logic but by song. Listen, and I will sing. And then Elihu does sing. At last we move into a totally new mode that is irrelevant to those scholars who want to continue to argue the issues.[70]

Biblical scholars have said that the text of Elihu is an interpolation that interrupts the story. So far as the original compiling of the story goes, they are right. Yet in the way they mean it they are so wrong.[71] Of course, it is an interruption of the legalistic approach to life that has dominated the dialogues. It is an inspired editorial insight. It announces the radical new message that is delivered by the Book of Job.

What is new, and absolutely central to the book, is the shift from argument as a mode of teaching to direct revelation through song and poetry. It is incredible but true that there are still commentators who view the poetic quality of the text as a decorative veneer.[72] Instead of listening to the music of song and poem, such a reader insists on the old categories and modes of inquiry. From such a standpoint God's words from the whirlwind can plausibly be characterized as a "complete evasion of the issue as Job posed it. . . ."[73] Indeed one commentator has argued that the Lord so patently fails to refute Job's arguments as to make Yahweh the butt of the reader's ridicule![74]

Elihu sings[75] of rains and storms that herald the winter, of the snow, ice, and hail that lead all creatures to withdraw into their dens, and then of the dazzling sun and hot winds of summer. Thus, abandoning argument, Elihu sings climactically of the radiant light streaming from the northern sky and of the splendor of God.

Then suddenly, without warning, out of nowhere, there is a thundering, shaking, shattering, cataclysmic whirlwind. The King James translation says that God "answered Job out of the whirlwind."[76] The Hebrew word refers to a rare but terrible tempest of thunder and lightning, great blasts of wind, clouds, and earthquakes. This phenomenon is associated in Hebrew literature with the appearance of God.[77] Elihu disappears from the scene as abruptly and mysteriously as he arrived.[78] It is the Voice of Existence that thunders.

Existence does not argue, debate, reason, or adjudicate. It makes no contracts. It issues no commands and promises nothing. It simply is. Of course, if we read the words of this Voice as if we were reading an argument or debate, it seems both bullying and irrelevant.[79]

But the Voice out of the whirlwind constitutes one of the great poems of literature.[80] It is not a description but a poetic revelation. It is a revelation of the glories, the wonders, the powers, and the mysteries of existence. It reveals order and harmony, and it also confronts Job with the wildness, and the amazing multifariousness of untamable existence. The Book of Job shatters the idea that the law is rooted in the divine or in the ultimate nature of existence.

Job is confronted with the absurdity of the idea that the Lord is constrained by any kind of law. Indeed the Voice at times ridicules Job for his belief. The whirlwind passages are not a would-be lecture about the Divine; they are a poetic vision of the Divine.

We are nothing as measured against the whole; we are puny, vulnerable, and transient. We can only be humble. But as beings who are conscious of this miracle of existence, beings who participate however humbly in it, we are like unto the angels. It is consciousness of the wonder of existence, not logic, that induces reverence. Authentic reverence compels utter truthfulness in one's stance toward what is revered. Job's reverence and truth before God now are lifted to a new and transcendent level.

"I abhor myself, and repent."[81] Such, at least, are Job's words as translated in the King James text. This rendering imposes a late Christian meaning on this pre-Christian text. The translation takes the harshest line. So far as the Hebrew text goes, the harshness is unnecessary and does not well reflect the original language. What Job actually says in the Hebrew text is more true to the situation: "I melt away, and I repudiate my words."[82]

The point is that Job does achieve humility; the self-assertive "I" has dissolved. But this humility is the very opposite of the humiliation that the King James text suggests. Humiliation presupposes an "I" that is assertive even in its impotence, an "I" that is coerced and self-denigrating. Such suffering is what we ordinarily recognize as suffering; it is misery. But authentic humility reflects neither impotence nor self-deprecation. It is as if the self-assertive "I" had been a cloud over the soul.

We can see an analogous loss of the self-assertive "I" in contexts other than the religious. What we feel before the sublime late quartets of Beethoven is humility, not humiliation. Authentic humility is never associated with being put down. When Beethoven's Opus 130 speaks to us, the "I" has "melted away."

Where the personal will is at last absent, suffering is complete acceptance. In a literal sense, it is suffering the reality of Opus 130 to be fully present to us.

Job's life is now newly and transcendently enriched. This inner transformation can only be expressed in metaphor. And that, of course, is how the Job story ends. This is accomplished with an epilogue in which we return to the simple language of the folk tale.

Job, we are told,[83] is now graced with redoubled prosperity. God gives him twice the cattle he had previously owned, three daughters, and (according to the Revised English Bible) twice the number of sons,[84] and one hundred forty years more of life. Each daughter is now gifted with surpassing beauty and a very substantial dowry.[85]

The Book of Job is thus not an argument but a book of transformed perspectives. As T. S. Eliot wrote, "Everything is true, but in a different sense."[86] Yahweh had said Job was an upright and blameless man. The satan charged that Job's blameless conduct was in fact motivated by self-interest. On the contrary, Job's blamelessness before God lay in Job's ultimate integrity, in the authenticity of his piety. The satan saw Job as deeply concerned with the good things of life; and the satan was right. This is evident in Job's glorying in the memories of his days of prosperity and his groaning over his loss of wealth, status, family, and health.

But what the satan did not realize was that when Job's integrity is at issue, all else becomes to Job as nothing. Job is unwavering in his refusal to abandon his integrity for the sake of getting back his prosperity. We now see that for Job, prosperity is the sign that he has been true to God and God to him. It is as such that he mourns his losses.

Paradoxically, at the end of the folk tale Yahweh says that Job has spoken correctly, and the friends have not.[87] For Job, unlike the friends, has addressed the Divine in the correct way, with utterly selfless commitment to truth. The friends have addressed the Divine in the wrong way. They have been smugly self-satisfied in assuming that they were in the right. They wanted Job to confess to sins he had not committed. In this they were in bad faith before God.

The Book of Job does not teach a negative attitude toward law. The message is that law and justice are matters of concern to humanity but not, in any ultimate way, to God. Or, to put this thesis in less theological terms, the meaning of human existence cannot be encompassed in terms of law and justice. These are truly important for human beings. However they are far transcended by the mysteries and many-sidedness of the creative forces of Existence. We need not diminish the importance of law; we need to magnify human existence.

Job had said "What is man, that thou shouldest magnify him . . . and that thou shouldest visit him every morning, and try him every moment?"[88] These words are answered by the words of the Psalmist: "What is man, that thou art mindful of him? And the son of man, that thou visitest him? For thou hast made him a little lower than the angels, and hast crowned him with glory and honour."[89]

Notes

Chapter 1: Accepting Responsibility

1. Kant, *Grounding*, 61.
2. Ibid., 648.
3. Ibid., 645–47.
4. See, for example, *Blocker v. United States,* the famous case in which several psychiatrists testified that Blocker was a psychopathic personality but that this did not entail that he was mentally disordered. The testimony allowed conviction of Blocker. Soon, thereafter, on a vote of the hospital committee, it was decided to classify psychopathic personality as a mental disorder. This led to a new court action based on the plea that Blocker was mentally disordered and therefore entitled to a verdict of "Not Guilty by Reason of Insanity."

Chapter 2: Guilt and Responsibilty

1. Freud, "Moral Responsibility,"133.
2. Freud, "Civilization and Its Discontents."
3. Paul, "Symposium," 214.
4. Fingarette, "Real Guilt and Neurotic Guilt."
5. Freud, "The Ego and the Id," 35.
6. Freud, "Analysis of a Phobia," 145 (emphasis in original).
7. Matthew 5:27–28.
8. Freud, "Notes Upon a Case of Obsessional Neurosis," 175–76.
9. Freud, "Civilization and Its Discontents," 137.
10. Hospers, "Free-Will and Psychoanalysis," 571 (emphasis in original).
11. Ibid. (emphasis in original).

Chapter 3: Orestes' Task

1. N. N. Dracoulides, "La généalogie des Atrides et l'adventure d'Oreste," *Psyche* 7 (1952): 805–17 and 8 (1953): 32–34; N. N. Dracoulides, "Profil psychoanalytique de Charles Baudelaire," *Psyche* 8 (1953): 461–85; J. Friedman and S. Gassel, "Orestes: A Psychoanalytic Approach to Dramatic Criticism, II," *Psychoanalytic Quarterly* 20 (1951): 423–33; J. Friedman and S. Gassel, "Odysseus: The Return of the Primal Father," *Psychoanalytic Quarterly* 21 (1952): 215–23; J. T. MacCurdy, "Concerning Hamlet and Orestes," *Journal of Abnormal and Social Psychology* 13 (1919): 250–60; G. Roheim, "The Panic of the Gods," *Psychoanalytic Quarterly* 21 (1952): 92–106.

2. Except where otherwise indicated, the quotations from Aeschylus are taken from the Philip Vellacott translation of Aeschylus's *Oresteia*. I have cited line numbers from the standard text format rather than page numbers since the latter vary from translation to translation. Unfortunately, Vellacott's translation does not provide the standard line numbers. Though I have quoted Vellacott's version for its poetic felicity, I have by no means relied on it for exegetical purposes. For these purposes I have relied on a wide variety of relevant texts, fully cited in the original published versions of this essay.

3. Aeschylus, "The Libation Bearers," lines 4–5.

4. Freud, "The Ego and the Id," 34.

5. Aeschylus, "The Libation Bearers," line 989.

6. Ibid., line 899.

7. Ibid., lines 900–903.

8. Freud, "The Ego and the Id," 39.

9. Freud, "An Outline of Psychoanalysis," 188.

10. Freud, "The Ego and the Id," 39.

11. Freud, "Remembering, Repeating and Working Through," 152.

12. Freud, "Introductory Lectures on Psychoanalysis," 331.

13. Ibid., 337.

14. Aeschylus, "Eumenides," lines 234–39.

15. Freud, "The Ego and the Id," 39.

16. Freud, "Introductory Lectures on Psychoanalysis," 337.

Chapter 4: Retributive Punishment

1. I am interested here in the issues, not the captions. The term "retributivism"—as with all such captions—has been used with differing meanings in the literature. Generally, the differences have lain not in incompatibilities of sense but in the decision as to which, out of a traditional repertoire of mutually compatible elements, shall be the elements actually incorporated in the particular user's def-

inition of the term. I have included all the key elements of the traditional reper-toire, minus question-begging or explanatory material; and I have omitted moral-istic language. Mundle also defends a "strong" version of retributivism ("Punishment and Desert," 221). And Mabbott ("Punishment") emphasizes the nonmoral basis of the retributive intuition. But most recent defenses have relied significantly on reducing the sense of the term to what is probably its bare mini-mal essential elements. These are that only the guilty may justifiably be punished; and that the need for retribution is to be explained on moral grounds.

2. Hart, "Postscript."

3. Fingarette, "Punishment and Suffering."

4. Kant, *The Metaphysical Elements of Justice.*

5. "Any retributive theory of punishment depends in some quite funda-mental sense upon the presence of a morally wrong act" (Wasserstrom, "H. L. A. Hart," 93.) See: Mundle, "Punishment and Desert," 221 and passim. Even Mabbott, in spite of his central stress on substituting a legalistic for a moralistic orientation, develops the plausibility of his own view by the use of moralistic analogies (e.g., promise keeping) and moralistic language (the judge "has no right to dispense from punishment") ("Discussion of Professor Flew on Punishment," 157). Mabbott adds that his own view is that the appropriate offi-cer "ought" to punish the offender, and relates this to the voluntary acceptance of the office, and the presumed value of the legal system. All of this reveals the underlying moralistic cast of even Mabbott's "pure" legalism.

6. Mabbott, "Discussion," 157.

7. In seeing this, I also saw at last the insight contained in the initially puz-zling theses of Hegel and Bosanquet that the rational criminal wills the punish-ment. See: Hegel, sec. 100; Bosanquet, 210–11.

Chapter 5: Alcoholism and Legal Responsibility

1. *Powell v. Texas* (1968). (Hereafter cited as *Powell.*)

2. Justice Marshall, joined by Chief Justice Warren and Justices Black and Harlan, held for affirming the conviction. Justice Black, joined by Justice Harlan, filed a separate concurrence. Justice White concurred in a separate opinion. Justice Fortes, joined by Justices Douglas, Brennan, and Stewart, dissented.

3. *Driver v. Hinnant* (1966).

4. *Easter v. District of Columbia* (1966).

5. *Traynor v. Turnage* (1988).

6. *Powell,* 560–61; *Driver,* 761–64; *Easter,* 53.

7. *Powell,* 567.

8. Ibid.

9. Ibid., 521.

10. Ibid.

11. I shall not further consider the trial judge's third finding since it does not bear on the general issues with which I am concerned.

12. For example, Dr. Wade, the expert witness, testified that individuals such as Powell have "a compulsion, and this compulsion, while not completely over-powering, is a very strong influence." *Powell*, 578, 559.

13. Ibid., 559.

14. Ibid., 559–60. All of the Justices seem to agree that medical knowledge of alcoholism is deficient. *Powell*, 522–23, 551 n. 3, 559.

15. Ibid., 559.

16. See the end of the following section, infra.

17. *Powell*, 568.

18. See the following section.

19. See, e.g., Plaut's *Alcohol Problems: A Report to the Nation*, 39.

20. *Powell*, 562.

21. *Fain v. Commonwealth* (1879). See also Morris, T., "Somnambulistic Homicide," 5.

22. Jerome Hall states that so far as case law is concerned, "involuntary intoxication is simply and completely nonexistent." See Hall, "Intoxication and Criminal Responsibility," 1056 (emphasis in original).

23. Plaut, *Alcohol Problems*, 41.

24. Jellinek, *The Disease Concept of Alcoholism*, 55–59, 83–86,113–15.

25. Block, *Alcoholism*, 23.

26. Chafetz, "Comment," 358.

27. Keller, "The Definition of Alcoholism," 313 (emphasis in original); Jellinek, *The Disease Concept*, 13–32.

28. See the discussion in Jellinek, *The Disease Concept*, 25–32.

29. Plaut, *Alcohol Problems*, 39–40.

30. Ibid.

31. Jellinek, in *The Disease Concept of Alcoholism*, says that 35% of the papers he has worked with that deal generally with the etiology of alcoholism use the term "addiction" or its foreign language equivalents.

32. *World Health Organization Expert Committee on Addiction-Producing Drugs, Thirteenth Report* (1964): 9–10. See generally Bowman, "Narcotic Addiction." Bowman's conclusions that only case-by-case analysis can establish nonresponsibility agree with those of *The President's Advisory Commission on Narcotic and Drug Abuse, Final Report* (1963).

33. *President's Advisory Commission on Narcotic and Drug Abuse,*13–16.

34. U.S. Department of Health, Education and Welfare, *Alcoholism* (1965). Merry reports his experiment in which alcoholics were given a daily dose of vodka, unknown to them, and who throughout the experiment were asked to report their "craving," if any, for alcohol. No deep craving for alcohol was report-

ed. In short, there was no physically induced "loss of control" among these alcoholics after the first drink. See Merry, "Loss of Control," 1257.

35. See Merry, "Loss of Control," 34.

36. "All addictive alcoholics do not always drink in an uncontrolled fashion." Pattison et al., "Abstinence," 610, 624.

37. There is no generally agreed upon or accepted etiological pattern in connection with alcoholism. There are many theories ranging from the physiological and the psychological to the sociological.

38. Jellinek, *The Disease Concept*, p. 43, note 44, alludes to the vagueness of the term "compulsion" as calling for caution in its use.

39. Pattison et al., "Abstinence," 525.

40. Forizs, "Who Is Qualified?" 510, 511.

41. Alcoholics Anonymous maintains that alcoholism is a "disease," but not that drinking is involuntary. On the contrary, the entire approach in Alcoholics Anonymous is to enlist the cooperation of the alcoholic to voluntarily abstain from drinking.

42. Hayman, *Alcoholism*, 174–75.

43. *Powell*, 560.

44. The new medical model treats alcoholism as a bona fide disease, without reservations. It enables those using it to draw strength from the successful campaigns against other major illnesses. Siegler, et al., "Models of Alcoholism," 584.

45. See, e.g., Jellinek, *The Disease Concept*, 161.

46. Ibid.

47. See ibid., ch. 4. See Hayman, *Alcoholism*, 81.

48. See Ullman, *To Know the Difference*, 4.

49. See, e.g., Fingarette, "The Concept of Mental Disease," 74.

50. Jellinek, *The Disease Concept*, 11–12.

51. Jellinek cites seven authorities who explicitly reject the disease concept of alcoholism. Ibid., 58–59.

52. For an ample review and bibliography on this topic, see the President's Commission on Law Enforcement and the Administration of Justice, *Task Force Report: Drunkenness*, 1967.

Chapter 6: The Concept of Mental Disorder

1. Spitzer et al., *DSM-IV Casebook*, 15–17.

2. The editors of DSM-IV state that "these diagnostic criteria and the DSM-IV classification of mental disorders reflect a consensus of current formulations of evolving knowledge in the field" (xxvii). "DSM-IV is used by clinicians and researchers of many different orientations (e.g., biological, psychodynamic, cognitive, behavioral, interpersonal, family/systems). It is used by psychiatrists,

other physicians, psychologists, social workers, nurses, occupational and rehabilitation therapists, counselors, and other health and mental health professionals.
DSM-IV must be usable across settings—inpatient, outpatient, partial hospital,
consultation-liaison, clinic, private practice, and primary care, and with community populations. It is also a necessary tool for collecting and communicating
accurate public health statistics" (xv).

3. Ibid., xxi.

4. Ibid., xxii.

5. Ibid.

6. DSM-I (1952)

7. "The current prevalence estimate is that about 20 percent of the U.S. population are affected by mental disorders during a given year" (U.S. Dept. of Health
and Human Services, *Surgeon General Report*, chap. 2). The *Surgeon General
Report* also states that 15% of the "life-years" lost to illness are from mental disorder—the second leading cause of such loss after the cardiovascular diseases. The
National Institute of Mental Health estimated that 44 million *adult* Americans suffer from mental disorder during any one year (NIH Publication 01-4584).

8. DSM-IV, xx.

9. Cf. Young, *The Harmony of Illusions*.

10. DSM-IV, xxi.

11. Cff. Szasz, *The Myth of Mental Illness*; Scheff; Becker, *Outsiders*.

12. Wakefield, "The Concept of Mental Disorder," and "Disorder as
Harmful Dysfunction" (and Horwitz, *Creating Mental Illness*, who accepts
Wakefield's concept) define mental disorder as "harmful dysfunction." That
is, mental disorder must, by definition, manifest two things. One is that the
conduct cause harm to the person's "well-being" ("The Concept of Mental
Disorder," 373). But, of course, harm alone is not enough since this is also
caused by many things other than mental disorder. The distinctive and really
operative word is "dysfunction." The latter, Wakefield defines as "the failure
of a person's internal mechanisms to perform the functions as designed by
nature . . ." (373).

This definition fails utterly on several counts. If adopted, it would require that
we know what "internal mechanism" failed to perform its function "as designed
by nature" and thus caused the harmful conduct. Yet rarely do we know what is
the internal mechanism that causes mental disorders, and perforce we cannot
know how that mechanism is "designed" to work. If this were so, it would follow
that DSM-IV has always been and remains largely guesswork! Psychiatrists could
not have discriminated normal harm from disorder-caused harm since they did-
n't, and usually still don't, know what those "internal mechanisms" are!
Furthermore, the notion that evolution has "designs" is radically inconsistent
with the scientific theory of evolution. The genius of the concept of evolution is
precisely that it explains the coming into being of highly complex structures without having to refer to some "design" or "purpose" of any kind. If, as Wakefield

argues, natural selection is the mechanism of "nature's design," then everything about us, whether we like it or not, whether harmful or not, whether "dysfunctional" or not, has survived natural selection. Hence, for example, so far as natural selection goes, schizophrenia, which has survived natural selection, therefore represents "nature's design."

13. DSM-IV, xxi.

14. Ibid., xxii.

15. Ibid., xxi. Emphasis added.

16. Ibid., 7.

17. Ibid. Emphasis added.

18. Ibid.

19. Ibid., xxi. Emphasis added.

20. Ibid., xxi–xxii.

21. Ibid., xxii. Emphasis added.

22. Ibid., xxi–xxii.

23. Cf. Horwitz, *Social Control*, chap. 2.

24. Fingarette, *The Meaning of Criminal Insanity*; Fingarette and Hasse, *Mental Disabilities*; Radden, *Madness and Reason*; Wolf, *Freedom Within Reason*; Morse, "Culpability and Control."

25. DSM-IV, xxiv.

26. Ibid., 9.

27. Ibid., 113.

28. Ibid.

29. All these items are to be found under the relevant headings in DSM-IV.

30. DSM-IV, 281.

31. Cf. Horwitz, *Creating Mental Illness*, 167–68. Horwitz provides a summary review of the incidence of schizophrenia across cultures. Especially when narrowly defined, schizophrenia is manifest at about the same rate in all cultures.

Chapter 7: Does Coercion Negate Responsibility?

1. Fingarette, "Victimization," 71 n. 17.

2. LaFave and Scott, *Handbook on Criminal Law*, 274 par. 49.

3. *Young v. Hoagland*, 431.

4. *Bram*, 542.

5. A classic expression of this dilemma was Lady Barbara Wooton's; in the nature of the case no proof of uncontrollability can be deduced, for ". . . no objective criterion which can distinguish between 'she did not' and 'he could not' is conceivable." Wootton, *Crime and Criminal Law*, 74.

6. Professor Abraham Goldstein's discussion of the conceptual difficulties associated with "irresistible impulse" and self-control issues remains an excellent overview. See Goldstein, *The Insanity Defense*, chap. 5.

7. *Bram,* 543.
8. *Culombe,* 576.
9. Ibid., 574.
10. *Great Northern Railway Co. v. State.*
11. *Wise v. Midtown Motors.*

Chapter 9: The Hindu Perspective

1. 4:16. The numerical citations in these footnotes refer to the standard notation of the chapters and paragraphs in the Bhagavad Gita. The translations used, and also the interpretations, are based on a wide range of texts as prime sources. I have either adopted the renderings, unaltered, from one of these texts, or have adapted and rephrased the passage on the basis of the comparison of English, French, German, and Sanskrit versions.

2. 4:18.

3. Some of these interpretations are descriptive; others are normative. The normative theses are propositions as to how one should act—act without attachment to the fruits, without desire, passion, or anger, with self-control, withdrawn from objects, with indifference to the opposites, performing acts as sacrifice. Of course, these propositions overlap in meaning, but they occur as reasonably distinct theses, and they are juxtaposed with the idea of actionless action in a way suggesting that they are explanatory of the latter theme as a normative principle. Descriptive meanings that can play an analogous explanatory role are, e.g.: (a) Our nature is essentially twofold, consisting of the embodied (*atman*), which is inherently nonacting, and of body or the field, with which action is associated. (b) When we act we are in fact driven to the act by the *gunas,* which are forces that have an essentially universal rather than uniquely personal character (3:5, 27–29; 18:19, 40–41). (c) When we act, our act is in fact shaped by influences arising inevitably from past actions, our *karman,* and in this regard our present action is not presently in our control. As I say in the main text, none of these theses is equivalent to the one I am presenting in this essay.

4. All these themes are akin to themes developed in chapter 11, "Responsibility and Indeterminism."

5. "Action" and "act" are in fact words that are typically used in more formal speech. In English we say "I did that" far more than we say "It was my action." The words "action" and "act" are often used with a special or technical meaning in such fields as law, drama, and philosophical action theory. In this study my aim is to stay close to English usage that is familiar, general, nontechnical. In the Sanskrit of the Gita, the relevant term, *karman,* has an overlapping but by no means identical range of connotations as compared to the English words "act," "action," and "do." In addition to connoting "action"

or "act" generally, *karman* may also connote specifically ritual acts. Or it may connote the doctrine concerning the effects of past actions. In the case of this crucial term, I have retained the traditional translation, the various forms of "action."

6. It will be noticed that, in the spirit of my approach generally, I also use the word "purpose" broadly, not technically. The one special or technical constraint arises in connection with what I call "executive purpose."

7. Let it be noted at once that "suffer" in the generic sense is not the same as Gita's term *duhkha,* which is closer in meaning but not identical to the narrow sense of "suffer," i.e., to suffer misery.

8. See Liddell, Scott, and Jones, *A Greek-English Lexicon;* and Renehan, *Critical Supplement,* 111.

9. There is a striking parallel in this regard between the experience of Arjuna during the theophany in chapter 11, and the experience of Job when the Lord speaks to him out of the whirlwind. Both texts are designed to exhibit how the vision of the Divine is inherently something suffered, something absolutely overwhelming, reducing one to absolute passivity (Job "I melt into nothingness")—and yet sublime. In the Book of Job, Job suffers miserably so long as he thinks that he can control and shape life by acting in certain ways. Then we see his new, insightful, blissful suffering when the Divine is revealed and he appreciates the absurdity of thinking of life in terms of human control. See the chapter on Job in this collection.

10. See the entry in the *Oxford English Dictionary.*

11. I have more fully developed aspects of this theme in two essays: one is the essay on Job included in this volume. The other is an essay not included in this volume. See Fingarette, "The Music of Humanity in the Conversations of Confucius."

12. 4:16.

13. 4:17.

14. "A self confused by consciousness of its own doings thinks, 'I am the doer.' What is done is done by nature, by the *gunas.*" (3:27).

15. "'I do not do anything'—thus steadfast in the discipline the knower of truth, whether seeing, hearing, touching, smelling, eating, walking, sleeping, breathing, talking, excreting, grasping, opening the eyes, shutting the eyes . . ." (5:8–9).

16. "Everyone is impelled to perform actions by the *gunas* . . ." (3:5). "All actions are performed by the *gunas.*" (3:27; and see also 3:28, 29). No doubt 3:33 should be read along these lines, even though the *gunas* are not mentioned as such. "There is nothing, either on earth or yet in heaven among the gods, no being, that can exist free from these three *gunas* born of Nature (*prakriti*)" (18:40). Book 14 is a lengthy disquisition on the specific natures and powers of the *gunas,* and books 17 and 18 contain much more on the topic.

17. Classic statements may be found in: *Brhadaranyaka Upanisad* 4:45; *Chandogya Upanisad* 5:10:7; *Svetasvatara Upanisad* 4:5:1:1–12. In the Gita, Krishna talks of it in 2:17–30 and 6:40–45. The notion of "rebirth" is mentioned in many passages in the Gita, wherein release from bondage to rebirth is declared to be the desideratum. In the history of Indian thought, the doctrine is developed and interpreted variously, though it is not much elaborated in the Gita. After several conferences over several years, in which much time was devoted to discussion of the topic of *karman* and rebirth, the conferees could make no more than an "ultimately vain attempt to define what we meant by karma and rebirth." (See especially O'Flaherty, xi.)

18. 3:27. The thesis, subscribed to by some scholars, that nature *(prakriti)* is to be understood as a materialistic system is controversial. The Gita explicitly includes the main psychic elements in *prakriti*. But inasmuch as mind is contrasted with matter in the European tradition, it would seem that a word like nature would be more suitable as a rendering of *prakriti*. This would allow for *prakriti* to include mind and matter.

19. Krishna's concluding words to Arjuna: "This wisdom have I told you; ponder it in all its amplitude, then do as you wish" (18:63). Zaehner reads 2:41–2 as saying that "the essence of the soul is will." Other major translators prefer "resoluteness," "sûre d'elle-même," "entschlossenheit," or "entschiedenheit." These seem to me more appropriate since the issue of freedom of the will does not enter here.

20. The same result obtains if instead of "initial purpose" or "executive purpose" one takes "character" or "desire and belief" as the crucial factors in action and examines them in a fashion analogous to that in which I have examined "purpose."

21. See, for example, Campbell's use of this important metaphor in "Has the Self Free Will?" in which he speaks of the "self" as the "author" of decisions and of acts.

22. 3:2–25. These express the idea that while Krishna need do nothing, he does act, and his action (as well as the actions of wise persons generally) is designed to "maintain the world order." So ritual action, action that constitutes maintenance of the world order, is proper action. Action that arises from personal ambition goes counter to this and results in both evil and "confusion." It is in this context, when referring to Brahman or Krishna as actor, that *karman* is spoken of as genuinely creative. "Action is known as the creative force that gives rise to states of being" (8:3). The key term, *visarga,* has the literal sense of "excretion," suggesting to the commentators "emission" in a sexual sense when used in the context of creation. See Zaehner's translation of the Gita, p. 280.

23. The most extended and eloquent statement of the case is found in 16:8–23, in which those who live for desire are portrayed by Krishna: "Clinging

to immeasurable anxiety, ending only in death, with gratification of desire as their only aim, convinced that this is all. '. . . I the enjoyer, I successful, I powerful, happy . . . I wealthy, I high born. . . .' Enveloped in a net of delusion."

24. Since "suffering" and the Gita's term *duhkha* are often equated, a few remarks are necessary to avoid some confusions. In some passages the Gita uses the word *duhkha* to refer to a specific content of experience. It is pain or other experiential content ordinarily valued negatively. Thus in 14:16 it is associated with passion, *rajas*. And in 6:22 we are told that the *yogin* is not shaken even by profound *duhkha*. This implies that it is an experience of the kind that would shake any but the disciplined. However it is an experience whose content does appear in the life of the *yogin,* though the latter is not shaken by it. On the other hand, 2:65 and 6:23 strongly suggest that the *yogin* is liberated from *duhkha*, freed from bondage to *duhkha*. Here *duhkha* has a different meaning. It is associated not with the content of the experience but with the spiritual attitude toward it. In this context *duhkha* is the effort to impose one's purposes on life; it is attachment to the fruits and the delusion that "I am the doer." Another way of interpreting the usage in these passages might be that although life inevitably brings us pain (*duhkha*), the liberated person is no longer in bondage to *duhkha*. This contrasts with the experience of the person who sees the meaning of life as consisting in the avoidance of pain and the achievement of *sukha,* happiness or pleasure.

25. "Not by abstention from action does a person get beyond action" (3:4). No one, not even for an instant, exists without acting. One is naturally impelled to act (3:5). See also 3:8 (we could not maintain the body without acting). "Therefore, letting scripture be your standard as to what is and what is not to be done . . . thou shouldst perform action here in the world" (16:24). The point that "renunciation" and "abandonment" do not mean the renunciation of all action but only of certain ways of acting is repeatedly emphasized in book 18, especially verses 2–12. "He, then, who is an abandoner of the fruit of action is called an 'abandoner'" (18:11).

Chapter 10: The Confucian Perspective: The Self

1. See, for example, *Brhadaranyaka Upanisad*. II 3.6; II 19:25; IV 2.4. References to classic works that exist in many translations but that have uniform chapter and paragraph notation are given simply with the name of the work and, if relevant, the standard numerical notation.

2. For examples of the doctrine of *sunyata*, see in Chan, *A Source Book in Chinese Philosophy*, chaps. 22–26. For examples from Indian Buddhism, see Conze, *Buddhist Texts*, 149–56. The *Heart Sutra* exemplifies this notion as found in the *Prajnaparamita* literature. See Conze, *Buddhist Wisdom Books*.

3. The doctrine of *anatta* (no-self) is distinctive of much Buddhist teaching. See, for example, Suzuki, *Lankavatara Sutra*, secs. 44–45. See also Conze, *Buddhist Wisdom Books*. For an example of a *Hinayana* text with this idea, see selection 66 in Conze, *Buddhist Texts*.

4. The teaching of *wu wei* appears early in Chinese thought as a central idea in the *Tao Te Ching* and *Chuang-Tzu* texts. The idea of "inaction in action" plays a key role in the great Indian text, the Bhagavad Gita.

5. See, for example, 1:1, 6:25, 7:8, 7:19, 7:33 in the *Analects* of Confucius. (In all the following citations from the *Analects*, I use the numeral headings used in almost all editions and languages.)

6. For example, 7:36, 13:26, 15:21.

7. For example, 2:10, 2:14, 6:3, 8:2.

8. For example, 4:5, 4:6, 4:10, 12:4, 14:1, 15:17.

9. For example, 4:16, 7:8, 8:13, 15:23.

10. 14:45.

11. *The Great Learning* (*Ta-Hsueh*), chap. 6. See also chap. 4.

12. The detailed analyses of the relevant text and key Chinese terms presented in the original published version of this essay are omitted here.

13. For example, 8:13.

14. For example,12:1.

15. For example, 4:5.

16. For a full discussion of Confucius's emphasis on these two principles as the "one thread" that runs through his teaching, see Fingarette, "Following the 'One Thread.'"

17. Creel, *Chinese Thought*, 36.

18. For example, 4:5, 4:16, 14:1, 15:31.

19. For example,1:1, 4: 5, 4:14, 8:13, 14:32, 15:18.

20. For example, 4:9, 9:17.

21. For example, 8:13, 14:13.

22. 2:1, and see 15:4. See the discussion in Fingarette, *Confucius*, chap. 1, note 16.

23. 4:13, 12:19, 13:16.

24. *Tao Te Ching*, chap. 49.

25. Ibid., chap. 7.

26. Ibid., chaps. 22, 34.

27. Ibid., chap. 17.

28. Ibid., chap. 20.

29. Ibid., chap. 14.

30. Bhagavad Gita, 5:8.

3l. Ibid., 5:10.

32. Ibid., 4:18–20, 18:23, 18:45–47.

33. *Analects* 8:15.

34. Ibid., 3:23.

Chapter 11: Responsibility and Indeterminism

1. Dennett says it would be "insane" to claim that a person could be morally responsible for an act where indeterminism intervened. Dennett, *Brainstorms*, 233.

2. For an extensive study of quantum physics in relation to questions of mind and consciousness, see Hodgson, *The Mind Matters*. A summary of recent experiments confirming action at a distance is reported in Schewe and Stein, "Nonlocality Gets More Real." Multidirectional time is discussed in "Competing Arrows of Time."

3. Rather than pretending to provide citations here that would constitute an unmanageable and unnecessary list, I refer the reader who wishes to review the history of attempts to explain free will to Ilham Dilman's comprehensive work on the topic.

4. The "passive aspect" that is discussed here was expounded at about the same time, though in very different contexts, in Dennett, *Elbow Room*, and in chapter 9 of this book.

5. See Danto, "Basic Action," 141–48.

6. With no pretense of covering here the large literature on this topic, it may be desirable to mention a few representative modern arguments for an uncaused will. See, e.g., Chisholm, "Freedom and Action," 23; Taylor, *Metaphysics*, 50–52; Campbell, *On Self and Godhood*, 156–57.

7. These are sweeping claims, and on the whole I can only refer the interested reader to the classic texts of any of these cultures.

8. Dilman concludes his account of free will along these lines, which he sets in a Wittgensteinian context. He develops this further in *Wittgenstein's Copernican Revolution*.

Chapter 12: Suffering

1. "The problem," said Eliot Deutsch, "is to determine the spiritual value of suffering" (*Religion and Spirituality*).

2. Spanish: *sufrir*; Italian: *sofirre*; French: *soufrir*.

3. Mark 10:14.

4. Spanish: *paciente*; Italian: *paziente*; French: *patient*.

5. *Tao Te Ching*, 3.

6. Ibid., 2.

7. Ibid., 7.

8. Ibid., 15.

9. Ibid., 19.

10. Ibid., 22.

11. Ibid., 43.

12. Hui Neng.

13. Bhagavad Gita, 4:18. (I have used Professor Deutsch's translations throughout.)

14. Ibid., 4:20.

15. Ibid.

16. Ibid., 4:22.

17. Ibid., 3:19.

18. 12:17–18. See also 14:24; 18:10.

19. Deutsch, *Religion and Spirituality*, 146.

20. Bhagavad Gita, 6:32. See also 14:24.

21. Ibid., 6:23.

22. Ibid., 6:22.

23. There are, indeed, some passages that may seem inconsistent with this oft-repeated theme in the Gita. Thus the Lord says at one point: ". . . one comes to the end of *duhkha*" (18:36). Read in context, however, this is a tautology rather than a substantive comment. In this passage the Lord is not speaking of the state of the *yogin* but is describing the respective kinds of happiness associated with each of the three *gunas*. Of course, when one is experiencing the form of happiness that is specific to one of the *gunas*, one is insofar not experiencing the relevant *duhkha*. Each of the *gunas* is associated with its specific form of *duhkha*, (18:37–39) for the *gunas* are associated with body (14:20). Only when the *gunas* are transcended is the body transcended, along with birth, death, old age, and *duhkha*, and thus immortality achieved (14:20).

24. "Review articles have generally found placebo effectiveness rates to be from 30% to 40%." Levin, "Placebo Effects," 1753.

25. I myself was once subject to a series of intense ("cluster") headaches that at first more or less immobilized me. Eventually I adopted a different attitude. Instead of fearing and fighting the pain, I simply let it be—it was there, but it was something toward which I took no stand. It was just a fact. Thereafter I could carry on, even when the pain was there, the very same pain as before.

26. *Meister Eckhart*, 87:246.

Chapter 13: Out of the Whirlwind: The Book of Job

1. See the discussion of Job, chs. 4–6, 8–9, 13–16, 19, 23, and 31 in Driver and Gray, *A Critical and Exegetical Commentary on the Book of Job;* in Pope, *Job;* and in Habel, *The Book of Job.*

2. E.g., Deuteronomy 12–25 (specific laws stated); Isaiah 42:6 (God's reasons for giving his law to the Chosen People of Israel).

3. I have not seen any work that takes up the theme of law in Job and treats that theme with any extended analysis. The major commentaries on Job go no

farther in an analytical direction than to remark briefly to the effect that Job talks in terms of bringing God to court, or of forcing God to acquit him. Many commentaries take up the doctrine of retribution and the theme of punishment and reward, but they do so only to report that Job learns the falseness of this doctrine. Little or no analysis is offered.

4. "It will be almost universally agreed that in the Book of Job we have the supreme literary masterpiece of the Hebrew genius," says Robinson, who alludes to it as possibly being "second to none in all the range of human writing" (*The Poetry of the Old Testament*, 67). Gordis characterizes the Book of Job as "the crowning masterpiece" of the Bible, and speaks of "untold readers and scholars who have recognized in it one of the supreme human masterpieces" (*The Book of God and Man*, 1, 3).

5. See ch. 2 in C. J. Friedrich, *The Philosophy of Law*.

6. One of the best known texts is that of the so-called "Babylonian Job," also known as "The Poem of the Righteous Sufferer," or "I will Praise the Lord of Wisdom." See Pritchard, *The Ancient Near East*.

7. Pope, *Job*, i–lxiv; Gordis, *The Book of God and Man*, ch. 5; Snaith, *The Book of Job*.

8. See Friedrich, *The Philosophy of Law in Historical Perspective*, 8.

9. Exodus 19.

10. See Dhorme, *A Commentary*, cxxvii–cxxx; Pope, *Job*, lvii.

11. See Friedrich, *The Philosophy of Law*, ch. 6 on Aquinas and ch. 2 on Calvinism.

12. See Fingarette, "Punishment and Suffering."

13. See note 7.

14. Eliphaz: "What innocent man has ever perished? . . . Those who plough mischief and sow trouble reap as they have sown; they perish at the blast of God . . ." New English Bible, Job 4:7–9. Bildad: "If you are innocent and upright, then indeed will he watch over you and see your just intent fulfilled . . . your end will be great. . . . The godless man's life-thread breaks off. . . . God will not spurn the blameless man, nor will he grasp the hand of the wrongdoer." Job 8:6–20. Zophar: "If you have wrongdoing in hand, thrust it away; let no iniquity make its home with you. . . . Blindness will fall on the wicked; the ways of escape are closed to them, and their hope is despair." Job 11:14–20.

15. "O that the grounds for my resentment might be weighed, and my misfortunes set with them on the scales." Job 6:2–3 (New English Bible). "Let me have no more injustice . . . for my integrity is in question. Do I ever give voice to injustice?" Job 6:28–30. " I will . . . take my life in my hands. If he would slay me I would not hesitate; I should still argue my cause to his face. This at least assures my success, that no godless man may appear before him. . . . Be sure of this: Once I have stated my case I know that I shall be acquitted." Job 13:13–18.

16. Good has stressed this idea: "We could say that the book shows Job's movement from a position of magical dogmatism [i.e., that man can by his excel-

lence require God to save and accept him or by his unworthiness require God to damn and reject him] to his ultimate stance in faith" (*Irony*, 197–8).

17. Job 38:2.

18. Habel, *The Book of Job*, 11. See Driver and Gray, introduction, § 7, *A Critical and Exegetical Commentary*; Dhorme, *A Commentary*, chs. 7 and 12; and Rowley, *Job*, 8–18. Pope says that the Book of Job "presents formidable linguistic and philological problems" (*Job*, xlii).

19. At this early period in Biblical history, the satan was the term for a roving spy for the king. The satan was also the accuser or prosecutor, and even an agent provocateur. See Habel, *The Book of Job*, 17.

20. Job chaps. 1–2.

21. Job 1:8–10.

22. Job 1:11.

23. Job 2:5.

24. Deuteronomy 10:12–13 (New English Bible).

25. But this issue has commonly been overlooked, in part for the reasons discussed in the text accompanying note 27.

26. Job 1:21 (New English Bible).

27. Most of the commentators have understood the main theme of the entire book to be the same as the characters in the dialog understand it. See, e.g., Pope, *Job*, lxviii–lxxv; Dhorme, *A Commentary*, cl–cli; Rowley, *Job*, 19–21; Driver, *An Introduction*, 409; Gordis, *The Book of God and Man*, 149; Driver and Gray, *A Critical and Exegetical Commentary*, liii–lxiii; Terrien, "The Yahweh Speeches," 497.

28. Job 4.

29. Eliphaz says, "Think how once you encouraged those who faltered. . . . But now that adversity comes upon you, you lost patience . . . and you are unmanned." Job 4:3–5 (New English Bible). "For my part, I would make my petition to God and lay my cause before him. . . ." Job 4:8, 17.

30. E.g., Job 4:8, 17. Eliphaz says, "Can mortal man be more righteous than God?" The word "righteous" in the Hebrew text connotes "on the right side of the law" or "having the law on one's side." Dhorme, commenting on Job 9:15, says, "The verb . . . 'to be righteous' . . . has equally the sense of 'to be in the right' in a debate or a lawsuit" (*A Commentary*, 145).

31. Job 15:4–6.

32. Job 8:8; 15:10.

33. Job 5:8; 17–18; 8:5; 11:13–15, 22:21.

34. Job 6:2–3. In later passages, Job further expresses his faith that if he could indeed bring his cause to trial and present his defense, God would surely acquit him. Also see 19:25–27; 23:2–7; 31:2–6; 31:35–37.

35. Job 6:4; 7:13–21; 9:16–20; 19:6–12.

36. Job 3; 7:15–16.

37. Job 6:14–27.

38. Job 6:28–30; 13:15; 27:2–6, 31.

39. Job 13:1–12.

40. Job 22:5–9.

41. Job 21:7–17. In Job 24:2–17, there is an eloquent portrait of the exploitation of the poor and innocent by the wicked. Plainly, Job and his friends see the problem as the meaning of suffering. This is the problem that most commentators also take as central to this work. But, as I argue in this essay, that view is mistaken.

42. Job 9:3 (New English Bible) (alternatively: "Man cannot answer God."); Job 9:19 (New English Bible): "Who can compel him to give me a hearing?" (King James: "[W]ho shall set me a time to plead?"). According to Dhorme, the language used here "assumes a juridical implication, 'summon,' 'cite,' before a court of law" (*A Commentary*, 138).

43. "[T]ell me the ground of the complaint against me." Job 10:2–7 (New English Bible). "[L]et me know my offences." Job 13:22–23 (New English Bible). "If my accuser had written out his indictment . . . I would plead the whole record of my life and present that in court as my defence." Job 31:35–37 (New English Bible).

44. "How much less shall I answer him, and choose out my words to reason with him?" Job 9:14 (King James). Dhorme says that the choice of the Hebrew term "to choose words" indicates concern for "the words which the accused would use before a tribunal" (*A Commentary*, 135). Pope, who translates the term as "match my words," also says the Hebrew word "is often used as a juridical term" (*Job*, 70). Another legalistic phrase, "[i]f I summoned and he responded," appears in Job 9:16a (New English Bible).

45. Job 16:21.

46. "For he is not a man, as I am, that I should answer him, and we should come together in judgment. Neither is here any daysman betwixt us, that might lay his hand upon us both." Job 9:32–33. The term used in the New English Bible and by Dhorme is "arbitrator." Pope uses "umpire." The custom was that by laying hands on the shoulders of the parties, the arbitrator or judge assumed jurisdiction over the case. See Dhorme, *A Commentary*, 144.

47. "For in my heart I know that my vindicator lives." Job 19:25 (New English Bible). The Hebrew word translated as "vindicator" is *goel*. The *goel* is an avenger, redeemer, or ransomer, originally the nearest kinsman who acts to avenge or ransom a member of the family.

48. Job 10:8–18. The concluding verses of Job's great oath in chapter 31 of the Book of Job are an eloquent summation of this attitude. It shows his ringing confidence in the justice of his claim. Nevertheless, there is the background of his despair that God will ever answer his appeal and acknowledge its justice.

49. Job 7:17.

50. Psalms 8:4–5.

51. Deuteronomy 10:11–13.

52. See Fingarette, "Punishment and Suffering."

53. Ibid.

54. James 5:11.

55. Job 23:13–14

56. Job 23:8–9.

57. Job 31.

58. Job 34:5–7.

59. Job 9:20.

60. Job 35:5–7.

61. Job 35:8.

62. "[M]an learns his lesson on a bed of pain. . . ." Job 33:19.

63. "[H]is soul draws near to the pit, his life to the ministers of death. Yet if an angel, one of thousands, stands by him, a mediator between him and God . . . if he speaks in the man's favour . . . then that man will grow sturdier than he was in youth." Job 33:22–25 (New English Bible).

64. See note 47.

65. Fingarette, "Punishment and Suffering."

66. Job 4:12–21.

67. Job 7:13–14.

68. "In dreams, in visions of the night, when deepest sleep falls upon men . . . God makes them listen . . . strikes them with terror . . . to check the pride of mortal man." Job 33:15–17 (New English Bible).

69. There is debate among authorities on the Hebrew text of 35:10 in the Book of Job as to whether the passage should read, as in the New English Bible, "But none of them asks, Where is God my Maker, who gives protection by night?" The King James version translates the passage, "But none saith, Where is God my maker, who giveth songs in the night?" The problem arises because there are two very similar root-forms, one meaning to "make music," and the other meaning "strong," "protect," "mighty." Compare the commentaries on this passage of Dhorme, Driver and Gray, Gordis, and Rowley, with that of Pope. Regardless of whether the poet had "song" or "support" uppermost in his mind, the two senses reinforce each other wonderfully. It is song and vision rather than physical might or legal reasoning that are the means for receiving God's strength.

70. Job 36:26 et seq. It is true that the New English Bible reads the hortatory phrase of Elihu at 37:14 as "Listen, Job, to this argument. . . ." But all other versions merely have "listen" or "hear." The insertion of the word "argument" in the New English Bible seems to be an interpretative elaboration which I believe misrepresents the message of the end of Job.

71. Certainly the Elihu speeches are an editorial interpolation. Elihu appears out of nowhere and disappears into nowhere. No one else ever alludes to him or to what he has said. But the appearance and the utterances of Elihu are integral to the aesthetic and religious meaning of the Book of Job. In Elihu we have the

crucial link. His song moves Job and us from the dead-end of Job's legalistic attitude to a new stance, rooted in suffering, song, and visions.

72. Kahn acknowledges that Job's ". . . language is appropriate to the intensity of the emotion which is being experienced," but prefers a psychiatric analysis which will give us "a modern perspective" on Job's "symptoms" (*Job's Illness*, 24).

73. Pope, *Job*, lxxv. Pope says this "must be the poet's oblique way of admitting that there is no satisfactory answer available to man, apart from faith."

74. Robinson, *The Poetry of the Old Testament*, 468. Robinson also says, "It is clear that in these two speeches [by Yahweh, out of the whirlwind] God is trying to convince Job and us of his innocence, that is, of the fact that he is a wise and just ruler of his world." Ibid., 462. But Yahweh's words and tone speak eloquently to the irrelevance of the issue of justice as it is raised by Job. The fact that Yahweh does not offer arguments designed to meet Job's case head-on implies that God takes Job's charges to be irrelevant.

75. "Remember then to sing the praises of his work." Job 36:24 (New English Bible).

76. Job 38:1 (New English Bible).

77. See Psalms 18; Habakkuk 3; Nahum 1:3; Zechariah 9:14; Ezekiel 1:4. See also Terrien, "The Yahweh Speeches," 500, n.4.

78. The Elihu text is an interpolation. Yet, from an aesthetic and religious standpoint, the interpolation is supremely apt. It fits his role as a transitional figure. When all hope is lost, he intercedes. . But he does not argue. He makes cryptic remarks to Job, and sings the praises and wonders of the Lord. It is common for such intermediaries in religious and spiritual crises to appear from outside, perform their role, and disappear again. It is a role well established in a number of traditions, from that of the psychoanalytic therapist to that of the boddhisattva in Mahayana Buddhism. See Fingarette, *The Self in Transformation*, chap. 6 .

79. Archibald MacLeish portrays Job as the moral victor over a tyrant god. Macleish's Job cries out, "I will not duck my head again to thunder—that bullwhip crashing at my ears. . . . Neither the Yes in ignorance . . . the No in spite . . . neither of them!" *J.B.*, 106–7. Jung took a similar view of Yahweh as the amoral bully-tyrant. See *Answer to Job*, chap. 2. And Kallen concludes that in the Book of Job God's "justice is his wisdom, and this again is nothing else than power, force, the go and potency, generative and disintegrative, in things. It possesses nothing of the moral or the human . . ." (*The Book of Job as a Greek Tragedy*, 71).

80. It is true that the magnificence of Job's poetry, and especially of the Yahweh passages from the heart of the tempest, has been widely acknowledged. But it is treated as if its ideas could be extracted for logical analysis, while the rest is merely poetic decoration. However the poet presents not arguments but images. I choose at random two out of innumerable amazing ones: "Canst thou bind the sweet influences of Pleiades, or loose the band of Orion?" Job 38:31 (King James). "Canst thou send lightnings, that they may go, and say unto thee,

Here we are?" Job 38:35 (King James). The commentators betray the work what by stripping off the "decorative" language. They take the message to be: "Are you as powerful or knowledgeable as I am? No!" One might as well discuss the meaning of Shakespeare on the basis of plot summaries.

81. Job 42:6 (King James).

82. The New English Bible reads, "I melt away; I repent. . . ." There are differences as to how to render this passage, the idea of "melting away" or "sinking away" being one possible rendering, favored, for example, by Dhorme. The rendering "abhor myself" is common. However in several of the principal early texts the verb has no object, the word "myself" being an interpretative elaboration. Pope says the verb in question is not used in terms of self-loathing and that the object of the verb is not "myself" but "my words." He translates the word as "recant." Terrien translates it as "I lose myself into nothing." He says that the Hebrew word used here, which is usually translated as "repent," has the meaning of intense pain at the thought of displeasing another. Terrien also says that the idea expressed is, specifically, that of "dying to his old self" and later refers to the "evocation of self-death" in Job 40:6. See Terrien, "The Yahweh Speeches," 505, 507. What seems most plain is that there is recantation, repentance, or self-humbling. What is most doubtful is that there is self-abhorrence.

83. Job 42:10.

84. Job 42:13.

85. Job, chap. 42, epilogue.

86. "The Family Reunion," part 2, scene 2.

87. Job 42:7–9.

88. Job 7:17–18.

89. Psalms 8:4–5.

Bibliography

Aeschylus. "Eumenides." In Aeschylus, *Oresteia.*

———. "The Libation Bearers." In Aeschylus, *Oresteia.*

———. *Oresteia.* Translated by Philip Vellacott. New York: Penguin, 1956.

American Psychiatric Association. *Diagnostic and Statistical Manual of Mental Disorders,* 1st ed. (DSM). Washington, D.C.: American Psychiatric Association, 1952.

American Psychiatric Association. *Diagnostic and Statistical Manual of Mental Disorders,* 4th ed. (DSM-IV). Washington, D.C.: American Psychiatric Association Press, 1994.

American Psychiatric Association. *Diagnostic and Statistical Manual of Mental Disorders,* 4th ed., text revision (DSM-IV-TR). Washington, D.C.: American Psychiatric Association Press, 2000.

Becker, Howard S. *Outsiders.* New York: Free Press, 1963.

The Bhagavad Gita. Translated by Eliot Deutsch. New York: Holt, Rinehart and Winston, 1968.

The Bhagavad-Gita. Translated by R. C. Zaehner. New York: Oxford University Press, 1976.

Block, Marvin. *Alcoholism, Its Facets and Phases.* New York: John Day Co., 1965.

Blocker v. United States, 288 Federal Reports, 2d Series 853 (1961).

Bosanquet, B. *The Philosophical Theory of the State.* 1923.

Bowman, A. M. "Narcotic Addiction and Criminal Responsibility under Durham." *Georgia Law Review* 53 (1965).

Bram v. United States, United States Reports, vol. 168, p. 542 (1897).

Campbell, C. A. *On Self and Godhood.* London: George Allen & Unwin, 1957.

Chafetz, M. E. "Comment: Who Is Qualified to Treat the Alcoholic?" (Comment on Krystal-Moore Discussion.) *Quarterly Journal Studies on Alcohol* 25 (1964): 358.

Chan, Wing-tsit. *A Source Book in Chinese Philosophy.* Princeton, NJ: Princeton University Press, 1963.

Chisholm, R. M. "Freedom and Action." In *Freedom and Determinism*, edited by K. Lehrer. New York: Random House, 1966.

Colombe v. Connecticut, United States Reports, vol. 367, p. 568 (1961).

"Competing Arrows of Time." *Physical Review Letters*, December 27, 1999.

Conze, Edward. *Buddhist Texts through the Ages*. New York: Philosophical Library, 1954.

————, trans. *Buddhist Wisdom Books*. London: G. Allen and Unwin, 1958.

Creel, H. G. *Chinese Thought from Confucius to Mao Tse-Tung*. New York: Mentor, 1953.

Danto, Arthur. "Basic Action." In *The Philosophy of Action*, edited by A. R. White. Oxford: Oxford University Press, 1968.

Dennett, D. C. *Brainstorms*. Montgomery, VT: Bradford Books, 1978.

————. *Elbow Room*. Cambridge, MA: MIT Press, 1984.

Deutsch, Eliot. *Religion and Spirituality*. Albany, NY: State University of New York Press, 1995.

Dhorme, E. *A Commentary on the Book of Job*. London: Nelson, 1967.

Dilman, Ilham. *Free Will*. London: Routledge, 1999.

————. *Wittgenstein's Copernican Revolution: The Question of Linguistic Idealism*. Swansea Studies in Philosophy. New York: Palgrave Macmillan, 2002.

Driver, S. R. *An Introduction to the Literature of the Old Testament*. New York: Meridian Books, 1960.

Driver, S. R. and G. B. Gray. *A Critical and Exegetical Commentary on the Book of Job*. New York: C. Scribner's & Sons, 1921.

Driver v. Hinnant, 356 Second Series Federal Reporter 761, 105 (1966).

DSM. *See* American Psychiatric Association.

DSM-IV. *See* American Psychiatric Association.

DSM-IV-TR. *See* American Psychiatric Association.

DSM-IV Casebook. *See* Spitzer et al.

DSM-IV-TR Casebook. *See* Spitzer et al.

Easter v. District of Columbia, 361 Federal Reporter 50, 106 (1966).

Eckhart. *Meister Eckhart: A Modern Translation*. Translated by Raymond B. Blakney. New York: Harper & Bros., 1957.

Eliot, T. S. "The Family Reunion." In *Complete Poems and Plays*. New York: Harcourt Brace, 1950.

Eliot, T. S. "The Family Reunion." Part 2, scene 2. In *Complete Poems and Plays*. London: Faber, 1969.

Fain v. Commonwealth, 78 Court of Appeals 183 (1879).

Fingarette, H. *Confucius: The Secular as Sacred*. New York: Harper, 1972.

————. "The Concept of Mental Disease in Criminal Law Insanity Tests." *Univ. of Chicago Law Review* 33 (1966).

————. Evans-Wentz Lectures in Oriental Religion. Stanford University, 1977.

————. "Following the 'One Thread' of the *Analects*." Paper presented at the Ancient Chinese Philosophy Conference, Harvard University, 1976.

————. *The Meaning of Criminal Insanity*. Berkeley: University of California Press, 1974.

————. "The Music of Humanity in the Conversations of Confucius." *Journal of Chinese Philosophy* 10, no. 4 (1983): 331–55.

————. "Punishment and Suffering." *Proceedings of the American Philosophical Association* (1977): 499–525.

————. "Real Guilt and Neurotic Guilt." *Journal of Existential Psychiatry* 3 (1962): 145–58.

————. *The Self in Transformation*. New York: Basic Books, 1963.

————. "Victimization: A Legalist Analysis of Coercion." *Washington and Lee Law Review* 42, no.1 (1985): 65–118.

Fingarette, H. and A. Hasse. *Mental Disabilities and Criminal Responsibility*. Berkeley: University of California Press, 1979.

Forizs, G. "Who Is Qualified to Treat the Alcoholic?: Comment on the Krystal-Moore Discussion." *Quarterly Journal of Studies on Alcohol* 26 (1965).

Freud, S. "Analysis of a Phobia in a Five-Year-Old Boy." In Freud, *The Standard Edition*, vol. 10, 5–149.

————. "Civilization and Its Discontents." In Freud, *The Standard Edition*, vol. 21, 641–45.

————. "The Ego and the Id." In Freud, *The Standard Edition*, vol. 19, 13–66.

————. "Introductory Lectures on Psychoanalysis." In Freud, *The Standard Edition*, vol. 16, 243–463.

————. "Moral Responsibility for the Content of Dreams." In Freud, *The Standard Edition*, vol. 19, 131–34.

————. "Notes Upon a Case of Obsessional Neurosis." In Freud, *The Standard Edition*, vol. 10, 158–318.

————. "An Outline of Psychoanalysis." In Freud, *The Standard Edition*, vol. 23, 144–207.

————. "Remembering, Repeating and Working Through." In Freud, *The Standard Edition*, vol. 11, 147–56.

————. *The Standard Edition of the Complete Psychological Works of Sigmund Freud*. 24 vols. Edited by James Strachey. London: Hogarth Press, 1955–61.

Friedrich, C. J. *The Philosophy of Law in Historical Perspective*. Chicago: University of Chicago Press, 1963.

Furman v. Georgia, 408 United States Reports 238 (1972).

Goldstein, Abraham. *The Insanity Defense*. New Haven: Yale University Press, 1967.

Good, E. M. *Irony in the Old Testament*. Sheffield: Almond Press, 1965.

Gordis, R. *The Book of God and Man*. Chicago: University of Chicago Press, 1965.

Great Northern Railway Co. v. State, Pacific Reports, vol. 93, p. 694 (1939).

Habel, N.C., ed. *The Book of Job*. New York: Cambridge University Press, 1975.

Hall, J. "Intoxication and Criminal Responsibility." *Harvard Law Review* 57 (1944).

Hart, H. L. A. "Postscript: Responsibility and Retribution." In *Punishment and Responsibility*. Oxford: Oxford University Press, 1968.

Hayman, M. *Alcoholism: Mechanism & Management*. Springfield, IL: Thomas, 1966.

Hegel, G. *The Philosophy of Right*. London: Oxford University Press, 1969.

Hodgson, David. *The Mind Matters: Consciousness and Choice in a Quantum World*. New York: Oxford University Press, 1993.

Horwitz, A. V. *Creating Mental Illness*. Chicago: University of Chicago Press, 2002.

———. *The Social Control of Mental Illness*. New York: Academic Press, 1982.

Hospers, J. "Free-Will and Psychoanalysis." In *Readings in Ethical Theory*, edited by W. Sellars and J. Hospers. New York: Appleton-Century-Crofts, 1952.

Hui Neng. *The Platform Scripture*. Translated by Wing-tsit Chan. Vol. 3 of the Asian Institute Translation Series, 1963.

Jellinek, E. M. *The Disease Concept of Alcoholism*. New Haven: Hillhouse Press, 1960.

Jung, C. G. *Answer to Job*. Translated by R. F. C. Hull. New York: Meridan Books, 1968.

Kahn, J. H. *Job's Illness: Loss, Grief and Integration—A Psychological Interpretation*. New York: Pergamon Press, 1975.

Kallen, H. *The Book of Job as a Greek Tragedy*. New York: Hill & Wang, 1959.

Kant, Immanuel. *Grounding for the Metaphysics of Morals*. Translated by J. W. Ellington. Cambridge: Hackett Publishing Co., 1963.

———. *The Metaphysical Elements of Justice*. Translated by John Ladd. The Library of Liberal Arts. Indianapolis: Bobbs-Merrill Co., 1965.

Keller, Mark. "The Definition of Alcoholism and the Estimation of Its Prevalence." In *Society, Culture, and Drinking Patterns*, edited by C. R. Snyder and D. J. Pittman. New York: J. Wiley, 1962.

LaFave, W. R. and A. W. Scott, Jr. *Handbook on Criminal Law*. St. Paul, MN: West Publishing Co, 1972.

Levin, M. R. "Placebo Effects on Mind and Body." *Journal of the American Medical Association* 265, no. 13 (1991).

Liddell, H. G., R. Scott, and H. S. Jones. *A Greek-English Lexicon*. 9th ed. Oxford: Clarendon Press, 1966.

Mabbott, J. D. "Discussion of Professor Flew on Punishment." *Philosophy* 30 (1955): 256–65.

———. "Punishment." *Mind* 48 (1939): 152–67.

MacLeish, A. *J.B.: A Play in Verse*. New York: S. French, 1956.

Merry, J. "The 'Loss of Control' Myth." *The Lancet* 1 (1966).

Moore, M. *Placing Blame: A General Theory of the Criminal Law*. Oxford: Clarendon Press, 1997.

Morris, Herbert. "Persons and Punishment." In *On Guilt and Innocence*, 31–58. Berkeley: University of California Press, 1976.

Morris, T. "Somnambulistic Homicide: Ghosts, Spiders, and North Koreans." *Res Judicatae* (1951): 5.

Morse, S. "Culpability and Control." *University of Pennsylvania Law Review* 142, no. 5 (1994): 1587–1660.

Mundle, C. W. K. "Punishment and Desert." *Philosophical Quarterly* (1954): 221.

O'Flaherty, W. D. Introduction to *Karma and Rebirth in Classical Indian Traditions*, edited by W. D. O'Flaherty. Berkeley: University of California Press, 1980.

O'Neill, Eugene. "Mourning Becomes Electra." In *Three Plays of Eugene O'Neill*. New York: Vintage Books, 1931.

Pattison, E. M., E. B. Headley, G. C. Glaser, and L. A. Gottschalk. "Abstinence and Normal Drinking." *Quarterly Journal of Studies on Alcohol* 29 (1968).

Paul, G. A. "Symposium on the Problem of Guilt." *Aristotelian Society Supplement* 21 (1974).

Plaut, T. *Alcohol Problems: A Report to the Nation*. New York: Oxford University Press, 1967.

Pope, Marvin H. *Job*. 3rd ed. Garden City, New York: Doubleday and Company, 1973.

Powell v. Texas, 392 United States Reports 514 (1968).

The President's Advisory Commission on Narcotic and Drug Abuse, Final Report (1963).

President's Commission on Law Enforcement and the Administration of Justice. *Task Force Report: Drunkenness*. Washington, D.C.: 1967.

Pritchard, J. B. *The Ancient Near East*. Princeton, NJ: Princeton University Press, 1969.

Radden, J. *Madness and Reason*. London: George Allen & Unwin, 1985.

Renehan, R. *Greek Lexicographical Notes. Second series. A Critical Supplement to the Greek-English Lexicon of Liddell-Scott-Jones*. *Hypomnemata* 74. Göttingen: Vandenhoeck und Ruprecht, 1982.

Robinson, T. H. *The Poetry of the Old Testament*. London: Duckworth, 1947.

Rowley, H. H., ed. *Job*. London: Oliphants, 1970.

Sartre, Jean-Paul. "The Flies." In *No Exit and Three Other Plays*. New York: Vintage Books, 1943.

Scheff, T. *Being Mentally Ill*. Chicago: Aldine, 1966.

———, ed. *Labelling Madness*. Englewood Cliffs, NJ: Prentice Hall, 1975.

Schewe, Phillip F., and Ben Stein. "Nonlocality Gets More Real." *Physics News* 399, October 26, 1998.

Siegler, M., H. Osmond, and S. Newell. "Models of Alcoholism." *Quarterly Journal of Studies on Alcoholism* 29 (1968).

Snaith, N. H. *The Book of Job, Its Origin and Purpose*. London: SCM Press, 1968.

Spitzer, R. L., M. Gibbon, A. E. Skodol, J. B. Williams, and M. B. First, eds. *DSM-IV Casebook*. Washington, D.C.: American Psychiatric Press, 1994.

———, eds. *DSM-IV-TR Casebook*. Washington, D.C.: American Psychiatric Press, 2002.

Suzuki, D. T., trans. *Lankavatara Sutra*. London: Routledge and Kegan Paul, 1932.

Szasz, T. S. *The Myth of Mental Illness*. New York: Hoeber-Harper, 1961.

Taylor, R. *Metaphysics*. New Jersey: Englewood Cliffs: Prentice Hall, 1963.

Terrien, S. "The Yahweh Speeches and Job's Responses." *Review and Exposition* 68 (1971).

Traynor v. Turnage, 99 L.Ed.2d 618 (1988).

Ullman, A. D. *To Know the Difference*. New York: St. Martin's Press, 1960.

U.S. Department of Health and Human Services. *Surgeon General Report: Mental Health*, chap. 2. Washington, D.C.: 1999.

U.S. Department of Health, Education and Welfare. *Alcoholism*. Public Health Service. Washington, D.C.: 1965.

Wakefield, J. C. "The Concept of Mental Disorder." *American Psychologist* 47 (1992): 373–88.

———. "Disorder as Harmful Dysfunction." *Psychological Review* 99 (1992): 232–47.

Wasserstrom, R. L. "H. L. A. Hart and the Doctrine of Mens Rea and Criminal Responsibility." *University of Chicago Law Review* 35 (1967).

Wise v. Midtown Motors, Northwestern Reports, 2nd Series, vol. 42, p. 404 (1950).

Wolf, S. *Freedom Within Reason*. Princeton, NJ: Princeton University Press, 1990.

Wootton, B. *Crime and Criminal Law*. London: Stevens and Son, 1963.

World Health Organization Expert Committee on Addiction-Producing Drugs, Thirteenth Report (1964).

Young, A. *The Harmony of Illusions*. Princeton, NJ: Princeton University Press, 1995.

Young v. Hoagland, California Reports, vol. 212, p. 426 (1931).

Index